Patrick Russell

A Continuation of an Account of Indian Serpents

Patrick Russell

A Continuation of an Account of Indian Serpents

ISBN/EAN: 9783742812278

Manufactured in Europe, USA, Canada, Australia, Japa

Cover: Foto ©Thomas Meinert / pixelio.de

Manufactured and distributed by brebook publishing software
(www.brebook.com)

Patrick Russell

A Continuation of an Account of Indian Serpents

A

CONTINUATION

OF AN

ACCOUNT OF INDIAN SERPENTS;

CONTAINING

DESCRIPTIONS AND FIGURES,

FROM

SPECIMENS AND DRAWINGS,

TRANSMITTED FROM VARIOUS PARTS OF INDIA,

TO

THE HON. THE COURT OF DIRECTORS OF THE

EAST INDIA COMPANY,

AND PUBLISHED BY THEIR ORDER, UNDER THE
SUPERINTENDENCE OF

PATRICK RUSSELL, M.D.F.R.S.

LONDON:

PRINTED BY W. BULMER AND CO. SHAKSPEARE PRESS,
CLEVELAND-ROW;
FOR G. AND W. NICOL, BOOKSELLERS TO HIS MAJESTY,
PALL-MALL.

1801.

EDITOR'S PREFACE.

T_{HE} present Fasciculus is the first of a projected Continuation of an Account of East Indian Serpents, begun in the Description of the Coromandel Collection lately published.

The Court of Directors considering it proper that an attempt should be made to complete the account of those pernicious animals, by inviting and encouraging research to be extended over the whole of British India, was pleased to transmit instructions to the Presidencies abroad, pointing out in detail the most probable means of success; and to render the conveyance of specimens, drawings, or other communications relative to Serpents, more easy, and less precarious, it was regulated they should be sent home, addressed to the Directors.

In these instructions, it was specially recommended to procure and send to the India-House, specimens in spirits, descriptions, and coloured drawings, of all such Serpents as were not comprehended in the Coromandel Collection; and that the Medical Board should be instructed to solicit the free communication of the cases of venomous bites, which future experience might furnish; as likewise the result of experiments made for discovering the properties of the poison, and the effects of medicinal applications.

An accurate discrimination of noxious from harmless Serpents, serves at the same time to lessen the prevalent terror of their poison, and to assist decision on the comparative merit of remedies employed: and whatever improvements may be expected in the medical treatment, must be ultimately established on the aggregate of facts gradually collected from extensive experience.

Descriptions and drawings, from living or recent subjects, made on the spot, are, no doubt preferable for ascertaining the species, to descriptions made from specimens preserved in spirits. But the former are not to be always expected. Of persons in India disposed to furnish specimens, some may harbour an aversion to handling even the dead reptile; others, through diffidence, may be unwilling to undertake a technical description: in either case, a well preserved specimen, with the aid of a few circumstances which may be easily collected, will answer the purpose.

The circumstances alluded to, are the following: the name of the Serpent in the vulgar language of the country; if rare, or common; its colour; its repute among the natives; the usual consequence of its bite; and what remedies are employed. The colour may sometimes be described in words; but, in many instances, the variegations can hardly be conveyed without the aid of a coloured figure: which, in cases where a better drawing cannot be procured, will render a mere sketch tolerably coloured, an acceptable substitute.

The Editor is led to insist on the advantage of drawings made in India, from the embarrassment he experienced in describing some of the subjects in the present Fasciculus, of which specimens only had been received, and where the change produced by the spirits, left the colour, in a great measure, to be decided by conjecture. To the Naturalist accustomed to specific characters reckoned less inconstant, a minute description of colour may be less requisite; but in common use, it will ever remain a material circumstance. In some hundreds of living Serpents which I had occasion to examine in India, the colour in individuals of the same species was found to vary less than the number of scuta or squamæ; and seemed to be less influenced by size, age, or situation, than I had been taught to expect: the tints were more or less vivid; the skin more or less glossy; but fillets, rings, and, in their general form, even spots, were found to maintain a characteristic similarity.

On a presumption, that having it sooner known in India what specimens had been received, might prove an encouragement for new contributions, the publishing in Fasciculi has been adopted, in preference to waiting till a number of specimens sufficient for a complete volume should be collected. But the promiscuous arrangement of the subjects of different genera, unavoidable in that mode of publication, will require a systematical index; in which also the Serpents of the Coromandel Collection are intended to be included: with as many of the native synonima of the whole, as can be procured. It is for this reason requested, where any of the subjects in the above collection, or in the published Fasciculi, happen to be met with under different names, that the new name may be transmitted for insertion in the projected index.

Besides the Serpents exhibited in the present Fasciculus, several have lately arrived from Bombay and Madras, and intelligence of several others has been received from sundry places, which may be expected in due time. A second Fasciculus may probably, therefore, appear early next year.

Where a specimen comes accompanied with a description and drawing, the Editor's duty will be restricted merely to correcting the press: nor will more be required for such facts or experiments as may be communicated in a form for immediate publication. In regard to medical cases of persons bitten, if related at length, it is proposed that brief mention of them should only be made in the Fasciculi; reserving the detail for an Appendix, where they can be arranged more advantageously for comparison with similar cases already collected. Of this kind, which justly deserve to be preserved, several have lately appeared in the India Newspapers, and in the printed correspondence of the Physician-General at Madras.

A description of the poisonous apparatus in Serpents, as also the result of some experiments made in India on their poison, may be found in the Coromandel Collection; and, to avoid repetition, the Editor takes the liberty of referring for other preliminary matters, to the Preface of that work, which is equally adapted to the present Continuation.

To conclude: it is with singular satisfaction he has remarked the subject of Serpents, within these last three years, to have been revived in India; and, from the abilities of many Gentlemen at present in that country, he is disposed to indulge strong hopes that the favourable opportunity now offered by the Court of Directors, will not be allowed to pass away unregarded; that inquiries will continue to be prosecuted with spirit; and that a too long neglected branch of Indian Natural History may soon, by united exertions, be highly improved: an event no less interesting to other tropical climates, than to the territories of the East India Company.

London, August 20th, 1801.

INDIAN SERPENTS.

No. I.

COLUBER.

Abdominal Scuta 185
Sub-caudal Squamæ 59 } 244
Coluber Naja, Linn. Syst. Nat. p. 382.

THE hooded snake, or Cobra de Capello, of the East Indies, generally reputed the most dangerous of the serpent tribe in that country, has of late been so amply treated of, in the Account of Coromandel Serpents, that referring to that work for a description of the Cobra, as also for the result of various experiments on its poison, it may be sufficient at present to offer some remarks of another kind, omitted before, on account chiefly of the want of an explanatory drawing, which my painter in India, (a native,) attempted unsuccessfully to execute.

The figure now presented is a sketch from life, by an English artist in Bengal, and exhibits the Cobra preparing for combat: his head and neck erected in a curve, resembling a swan's neck, are firmly supported by the convolutions of part of the trunk and the tail, while the hood is partially, not fully, expanded.

The gentleman to whom I am obliged for the drawing,* favoured me at the same time with the following remark.

" When the Cobra de Capello has raised himself for combat, he makes a full inspiration, by which the whole body being inflated, the scales are separated from each other, and the interstitial skin becomes visible from the head to the tail, but less and less in approaching the vent. On the succeding expiration, the body collapsing, the interstitial skin is no more visible, except on the hood and upper part of the trunk. In this manner, as the animal breathes, the body alternately swells and shrinks, but the hood and the neck remain expanded."

It may be further remarked, when the hood is expanded, the neck bent, and the nose pointing directly foreward, that no part of the head is visible to a spectator placed exactly behind : yet the head is not properly hooded, or concealed by the hood, and the scales in front, are not so much separated as on the back of the hood, which is somewhat convex.

---

* Mr. Alexander Russell of Bengal, a former contributor to the Coromandel Collection, and to whom acknowledgment is due for all the specimens contained in the present Fasciculus.

PART II.

In the exhibition of serpents, by way of show, by strollers in India who travel round the country, the Cobra de Capello makes a conspicuous figure, and, so far as I know, is the only serpent they pretend to charm by music. It is indeed the only venomous serpent I ever remarked in their collections, though sometimes consisting of more than a dozen of different species.

These itinerants are usually provided with pretended antidotes against poison, which they vend to the spectators; and, in proof of their boasted efficacy, will allow themselves to be bitten: but in such case, the fangs of the Cobra have commonly been eradicated, and where blood is drawn, the wound has been made by the common teeth, or holders.

The showman, placed on the ground, sits squatted on his hams, holding a reeden pipe in his left hand, which he begins to sound as soon as he has taken off the cover of the round flat basket, in which the serpent lies coiled up. At the sound of the pipe, or when less alert, excited by the touch of a small rod, the Cobra raising his head, assumes by degrees the attitude in which he is represented in the Plate. Sometimes he is shaken out of the basket, which makes no difference in his subsequent movements.

The serpent being erect, the showman commences what is called the dance, by a slow movement of his body sidewise to right and left alternately; varying the measure to the cadence of his music, and sometimes rising and sinking on his hams. The serpent, with eyes intently fixed on its master, imitates his gestures, but watches particularly his right hand, which, shielded by the lid of the basket, or sometimes naked and clinched, is now and then advanced in a hostile manner, to provoke the serpent to snap. The movements of the serpent are not devoid of grace, and afford some amusement; but being unable to sustain the exercise beyond a short time, it becomes necessary, when the exhibition is prolonged, to produce a fresh performer.

It need hardly be remarked, that the music of the pipe has no influence on a Cobra in its wild state. He is trained for exhibition by a course of severe discipline, of which a circumstantial account has long since been given by Kempfer.[*]

That bad accidents from the bite of the mutilated snakes commonly exhibited to the public, should not be oftener heard of, has been remarked on another occasion, as surprising.[+] But, though rare, they sometimes happen, and may easily be accounted for.

In the Account of Coromandel Serpents, more than a score of the hooded snakes, under different appellations, are mentioned as having been examined without discovering any specific character of distinction, or difference in the malignity of their poison. Since my return, however, from India, I have heard of a small Cobra de Capello, found in the vicinity of Benares, which seems, from the description, to be specifically different from any known on the coast of Coromandel; but a specimen being expected, a further account is reserved for a future occasion.

* Amœnitates Exoticæ, p. 569.   + Account of Coromandel Serpents, p. 11.

OBSERVATIONS.

I have before had occasion to remark, that the natives on the coast of Coromandel, distinguish a number of varieties of the Cobra de Capello, by different names ; but that I had found the distinctive characters extremely vague.*

The mark in the hood of the Coromandel *Coodum Nagoo*, is indeed very different from that of the others ; but slight variations, both in shape and colour, are met with in all of them.

The *hood* of the Sankoo Nagoo is plain, without any mark. From the specimen now in the Museum of the late Mr. John Hunter, it appears that Seba was mistaken in conceiving the want of the spectacle-mark to be a specific character of the female serpent.+ I am led to repeat this remark on observing that the mistake of Seba has been adopted by the Count de la Cepede in his Continuation of Buffon's Natural History.‡

Laurentius has made it a distinct species, calling it Naja non Naja.

In Gmelin's edition of Linnæus, the three following varieties of the Coluber Naja are adopted from Laurentius, and references made to the figures in Seba's Thesaurus.

1 Naja fasciata Seba Thes. Vol. II. Tab. 89. f. 3.

2 Naja Siamensis, ib. - - - - - - - - - - f. 1, 2.

3 Naja Maculata ib. - - - - - - Tab. 90. f. 2.

The Naja Brasiliensis of Laurentius, Seba, p. 96. Tab. 80, f. 4, is, by Gmelin, made a new species under the name *Rufus*.

The figure on the hood of that serpent, is certainly different from the others; but if sufficient to constitute a distinct species, would not the Coromandel Coodum Nagoo have the like pretension?

The two hooded snakes in Seba, the one from Peru, Thes. Vol. II. Tab. 85. f. 1, the other from New Spain, Tab. 97. f. 4, are treated of separately by Cepede, on a supposition that the skin of the neck was not (as in the other species) capable of expansion. But this can hardly be inferred from the words of Seba, " non huic majus ac cuicunque vulgari serpente tumet collum." Which may be equally said of all hooded snakes, when their necks are in a collapsed state.

As to the Cobra from Peru, in Seba, Tab. 85. f. 1, a more particular description is found in Gronovius.§ It has 193 Scuta, and 62 Squamæ ; and I should think there is no ground for suspecting it differs materially from the Cobra de Capello of the East Indies. The same may be said of Seba's serpent from New Spain, Tab. 97. f. 4 : by the way, the description of the mark on the hood of that serpent, (p. 103,) by no means agrees with the figure referred to.

It appears upon the whole, that the hooded snake is a native of the new, as well as of the old continent.

---

* Account of Coromandel Serpents, p. 7.   + Ibid. p. 9.
‡ Histoire Naturelle des Serpens, Tome II. p. 89. Paris 1789.   § Zoophylacium, p. 20. No. 96.

No. II.

COLUBER.

Abdominal Scuta   209 }
Sub-caudal Squamæ 129 } 338

Called by the natives, *Kalla Jin.*

The *head* broader than the neck, depressed, thin, ovate. The principal laminæ twelve in number. The one in front trigonal, somewhat emarginate ; the pair between the nostrils, orbicular ; the next pair square, and larger ; the central lamina between the eyes, small, trigonal, with a singular cordate appendage ; the lateral laminæ large, oblong-ovate ; the posterior pair semicordate with a pretty large lamina on each side.

The *mouth* large. The lower jaw a little shorter than the upper. A double row of palatal teeth, and a marginal row, above ; no fangs: the under teeth as usual.

The *eyes* lateral, nearer the rostrum than the angles of the mouth, large, oval. The nostrils lateral, very near the point of the rostrum.

The *trunk.* The neck small, round ; the back convex, the sides towards the scuta compréssed, the abdomen flat. The *tail* tapers to a very small, sharp, point. The scales ovate, smooth, imbricate: but those next the scuta, are larger and somewhat angular.

The entire *length* of the subject two feet ten inches, of the tail nine inches; circumference of the neck eleven lines, of the body one inch and a half.

The *colour.* This animal is singularly and beautifully speckled. The orange colour marks on the upper part of the polished black head, give it a resemblance to some species of beetle. Along the ridge of the back, from the neck to the end of the tail, is a row of orange yellow, crucial, spots, with oblique rows of short, straw-colour lines on each side. The ground colour is black. The scuta are of a yellowish white, with a black dot on each side of the margins.

OBSERVATIONS.

Allowance must be made in the colour, for change produced by the spirits ; the specimen not being accompanied with a drawing.

In the second Volume of Seba's Museum, this serpent seems to be described in two places. In p. 7. Tab. 7, under the name of Ibiboboca, from Brasile ; and in p. 60, Tab. 61. " Serpens Ceilanica pomposâ veste ornata."

No. III.

COLUBER.

Abdominal Scuta 151⎫
Sub-caudal Squamæ 93⎭244
Called by the natives *Dooblee.*

The *head*, a little broader than the neck, oblong-ovate, compressed. The two anterior laminæ between the nostrils trigonal; the next pair square, rounded behind; the middle lamina between the eyes lanceolate, those on the sides conical, convex; the semi-cordate lamina well shaped, large.

The *mouth* proportionally large. A marginal row of teeth above; no fangs.

The *eyes* large, orbicular. The *nostrils* small, very near to the point of the rostrum.

The *trunk* round, well shaped. The *tail* tapering, becomes very slender, and terminates in a long, sharp point. The scales, on the back ovate, carinate, on other parts smooth.

The *length* thirteen inches; of the tail, four inches.

The *colour* of the head light brown; the trunk freckled with dusky yellowish spots; the scuta a yellowish white, and most of them with black margins.

No. IV.

COLUBER.

Abdominal Scuta 154⎫
Sub-caudal Squamæ 67⎭221
Called by the natives *Chittee.*

The *head* oblong-ovate, hardly broader than the neck, obtuse, flattish on the crown, compressed on the sides. A single triangular lamina between the nostrils; the next pair orbicular, the middle lamina between the eyes broad, shield-form, the lateral conical and slightly convex; the semicordate pair sub-truncate, with an oblong lamina on each side.

The *mouth* middle size. A marginal row of teeth in the upper jaw; no fangs.

The *eyes* large, lateral, sub-oval. The *nostrils* small, on the edge of the rostrum.

The *trunk*. The neck and body round, swells towards the middle, and, as usual, gradually diminishes towards the anus; but the *tail* tapering rapidly, ends in a sharp point.

The *scales* smooth, ovate.

The *length* of the subject one foot seven inches; of the tail three inches, and three-fourths.

The *colour*. The crown of the head, and upper parts of the body, appear uniformly of a bluish clay colour ; the belly of a tawny buff.

No. V.

COLUBER.

Abdominal Scuta 135 ⎫
Sub-caudal Squamæ 73 ⎭ 208
Called by the natives *Dora*.

The *head* a little broader than the neck ; oblong, obtuse, compressed on the sides. The laminæ between the nostrils small, conical, the next pair orbicular ; the middle lamina between the eyes oblong, acuminate, the lateral sub-conical, convex ; the semi-cordate pair well shaped, rather large.

The *mouth* moderate size; a marginal row of teeth above; no fangs. Two front teeth in the lower jaw remarkably large.

The *eyes* small, globular. The *nostrils* close to the rostrum, small.

The *trunk*. The body round, regularly shaped ; the *tail* rather thick, tapering to a sharp point. The scales ovate ; on the back, in several series carinate, on other parts smooth.

The *length* of the subject described two feet two inches; of the tail seven inches and a half. Circumference of the neck, one inch and a half; of the thickest part of the trunk two inches and a half.

The *colour*. The head of a clay colour; the body much darker, and variegated with dusky-yellowish spots. The scuta and squamæ a yellowish-white.

No. VI.

ANGUIS.

Squamæ Abdominales 323 ⎫
Squamæ Sub-caudales 46 ⎭ 369
Called by the natives *Kerril pattee*.

The *head* very small, oblong, obtuse, slightly convex on the crown, flattish on the sides. The principal laminæ ten in number. The first, in front, trigonal, the point inserted between the next pair, which are oblong, square, and perforated by the nostrils; next to these a sub-orbicular pair; the central lamina of three between the eyes, orbicular with a sharp point ; those on the sides oblong ; the posterior pair rudely semicordate, and deeply divided at the base by the point of the central lamina.

The *mouth* wide, the jaws of equal length.   One, or more, very minute fangs are found on each side of the upper jaw, situated in the usual place.   There are no marginal teeth ; and the palatal, as well as the teeth in the under jaw, are remarkably small.

The *eyes* lateral.   The *nostrils* almost vertical, round.

The *trunk.*   The neck slender, hardly broader than the head, round, long ; the back rounded, the sides declivous, the belly carinated ; the trunk grows gradually thicker, till near the anus, where it diminishes a little.   The *tail* short, flat, round pointed, the edges very thin.   The scales imbricate, oval on the upper part of the neck, and smooth ; on other parts carinate; on the back ovate, on the sides and belly orbicular: the abdominal and subcaudal scales inconsiderably larger than the others.

The *length* three feet four inches; of the tail four inches and a quarter.   Circumference of the head one inch three lines ; of the neck one inch and a half ; of the thickest part of the body three inches three-fourths ; two inches from the vent, two inches one-third.

The *colour*, olive green above, yellow beneath, with 5 8 black, or dark-blue bands on the trunk, and nine on the tail.   These bands completely encircle the body, but are broadest on the ridge of the back, narrowing towards the belly.

OBSERVATIONS.

A fowl bitten in the thigh, very soon became disordered ; it drooped its head, and within a minute and a half showed other signs of infection ; at the end of five minutes, it was seized with convulsions, and in two minutes more expired: that is, in seven minutes after the bite.

This Anguis, and the four which immediately follow, were brought to Calcutta from the salt water rivers which intersect that part of Bengal called the Sunderbunds.

They were observed to be very alert and nimble while in water, but moved slowly on dry ground. Those who brought them, appeared ignorant of their being venomous. They said they were found only in salt water ; that they soon die, when taken out of the water ; and even in fresh water can survive but a short time: they added, probably with a view of enhancing the price, that they were very rare.

I must remark here, that all the specimens in spirits from Calcutta, being carefully put up, were received in good preservation, and four of them were accompanied with coloured drawings.

No. VII.

ANGUIS.

Squamæ Abdominales 332 ⎫ 372
Squamæ Subcaudales   40 ⎭
Called by the natives *Shootur sun.*

The *head* hardly thicker than the neck, extremely small, oblong, flattish on the crown and sides, obtuse. The larger laminæ twelve in number. One in front trigonal, convex, the pair next behind, oblong square, and perforated by the nostrils, the next pair orbicular; the central lamina between the eyes broad, pentagonal; the lateral, small, roundish; the semicordate pair long, with a thin lamina near the point, on each side.

The *mouth* large; the jaws of equal length. A small fang was found in the upper jaw, on each side, with three common teeth immediately behind them, disposed rather obliquely, in respect to the palatal rows. The rest of the teeth very minute, curve, reflex.

The *eyes* orbicular. The *nostrils* nearly vertical.

The *trunk*. The neck extremely small, long, round; the body disproportionately thick, the sides declivous, the belly carinate. The tail flat, somewhat curve, round pointed. The scales carinate, imbricate; ovate on the back, on other parts orbicular, those on the carina of the belly not larger than the others.

The *length* three feet eleven inches; of the tail four inches and a half; of the head, three fourths of an inch. Circumference of the head, one inch; of the trunk, where thickest, (in its collapsed state) four inches three-quarters.

The *colour*, a dark blue, intermixed with green. The neck crossed with bands of greenish yellow; and broader bands of the same colour across the sides and the tail.

OBSERVATIONS.

In the dimensions of this and the other subjects, allowance must be made for the change produced by the spirits.

A small specimen, measuring in length, one foot two inches one-fourth accompanied the large one. It was in every respect completely formed, and coloured like the mother; and one of nine which Mr. Russell found on opening her belly, each contained in a distinct egg.

The common teeth behind the fangs, in this and the three following subjects, is a very remarkable circumstance. The only instance I have ever met with of a similar anomaly in the teeth, was in the Boa, No. III. of the Coromandel Collection.*

* P. 5. The position of the teeth is distinctly shown in the Anatomical Plate, No. XLV. of that work.

No. VIII.

ANGUIS.

Squamæ Abdominales 338
Squamæ Subcaudales 48 } 386
Called by the Natives *Kalla Shootur Sun.*

The *head* small, a little broader than the neck, ovate, flattish on the crown and the sides. The front lamina trigonal; the pair perforated by the nostrils oblong, large; the next pair smaller, sub-orbicular; the central lamina between the eyes, short, resembling the point of a lancet; the lateral oval; the semicordate pair narrow, deeply cleft at the base, and several laminæ on each side.

The *mouth* wide; the under jaw somewhat shorter than the upper. There is a small fang on each side of the upper jaw, behind each of which, in a line more parallel to the palatal rows than in the preceding subject, are three common holders. The rest of the teeth are curve, as usual, but very small.

The *eyes* high, small, orbicular. The *nostrils* nearly vertical, large.

The *trunk*. The neck slender, round, swelling gradually into the body, which is rounder, and more proportionally shaped than any of the angues described in the present fasciculus; the back convex, the sides declivous, the belly carinated. The *tail* more curve and obtuse, than in the others, and much thicker in the middle, but the margins thin, as in them. Most of the *scales* carinated; on the neck oval, on other parts ovate, or orbicular, all imbricated: those on the belly not bigger than the rest.

The *length*, three feet eleven; of the tail, five inches and a half; of the head, three-fourths of an inch. Circumference of the head, one inch.

The *colour*. The neck a bluish black, with yellow bands; the back likewise of a bluish black, but some shades lighter; the sides and belly, yellow, encircled by faint darkish bands, to the end of the tail.

REMARKS.

No drawing accompanied the specimen of this serpent, and allowance should be made for alteration of colour produced by the spirits.

No. IX.

ANGUIS.

Squamæ Abdominales 308 ⎫
Squamæ Subcaudales   48 ⎭ 356

Called by the natives, *Chittul.*

The *head* small, in proportion to the length of the animal, hardly broader than the neck, oblong, roundish, obtuse. The front lamina trigonal; the first pair oblong-square, large, and perforated by the nostrils; the next pair sub-orbicular; the central lamina between the eyes lancet-form; the lateral sub-oval; the semicordate pair ill shaped, with some large scales on the sides.

The *mouth* small for the size of the subject. There are small fangs in the upper jaw, and behind them are four common holders, placed, as in the preceding, less obliquely than in No. VII.° The teeth are very slender and short.

The *eyes* high, small, orbicular. The nostrils on the verge of the declivity of the obtuse rostrum.

The *trunk.* The neck round, nearly of equal thickness; the body more round than in any of the preceding angues, till within ten inches of the anus, when, as in them, it becomes compressed; the belly is not carinated till near the tail. The *tail* flat, but shorter and less curve than in the others. The *scales* small, smooth, imbricate; orbicular on the sides, on other parts ovate; but those on the belly are orbicular with ciliated margins, and, in comparison with the other angues, much larger in size.

The *length* five feet; of the tail five inches; of the head one inch and a half. Circumference of the head two inches and a quarter; of the neck one inch and a half; of the trunk, where thickest, four inches and a half.

The *colour*, blue, with circular bands of yellowish white.

OBSERVATIONS.

A fowl bitten in the thigh by this serpent, expired in eight minutes.

* Vide p. 1.

No. X.

ANGUIS.

Squamæ Abdominales 306 ⎫
Squamæ Subcaudales 52 ⎭ 358

Called by the natives *Hoogli pattee.*

The *head* oblong, obtuse, bulges behind, and thicker than the neck. The front lamina small, but trigonal as usual ; the next pair, perforated by the nostrils, oblong, remarkably large ; the pair immediately behind similar in shape, but placed obliquely, and receiving between them the point of the middle oval lamina, of the three between the eyes ; the lateral sub-lunate ; in the centre of the semicordate laminæ, there is an uncommon oval one divided longitudinally, which, having been observed in several subjects, would appear to be not accidental.

The *mouth*, proportionally large. In the upper jaw, on each side, there is a small poison fang, behind which, placed obliquely (as in No. VII.[*]) are two or three common teeth. The palatal rows, and the teeth in the under jaw are small.

The *eyes* oval. The *nostrils* gaping.

The *trunk.* The neck roundish; the back rounded; the sides declivous, compressed; the belly carinate. The *tail* flat, curve, round pointed, the edges very thin. The *scales* ovate; on the back carinated and imbricate ; on the sides smooth, orbicular, contiguous, on the carina of the belly smooth, small, ovate, imbricate.

The *length*, three feet and half an inch ; of the tail five inches ; of the head one inch two lines. Circumference of the head one inch eight lines.

The *colour* of the head, back, and tail, blue ; the sides and belly pale buff.

OBSERVATIONS.

A fowl bitten in the thigh, by this reptile, expired in five minutes.

* Vide p. 1.

No. XI.

ANGUIS.

Squamæ Abdominales 318
Squamæ Subcaudales 45 } 363

Called by the Natives *Valakadyen*.

The *head* oblong, compressed, equally thick with the neck behind, but contracting as it projects into the obtuse rostrum. The front lamina (usually trigonal) is here round ; the pair immediately behind large, pyramidal, perforated by the nostrils ; the next pair nearly of the same shape, placed obliquely between the eyes and the nostrils ; the central lamina of the three between the eyes, small, round ; the lateral broad ; the semicordate pair well shaped on one side, on the other lacerated : the occiput covered with small orbicular scales, each having a raised point in the centre.

The *mouth* wide ; without fangs ; the teeth above and below extremely small. The *eyes* small, orbicular, high, lateral. The *nostrils* vertical, ringent.

The *trunk* cylindrical, of equal thickness throughout, or swelling a little at the middle. The *tail* short, double-edged, sword-form. The *scales* small, orbicular, hexagonal or oval ; in most parts rather contiguous than imbricated ; each scale has a small raised point in the middle.

The *length* three feet three inches, of which the tail claims four inches and a half.

The *colour*. The head and trunk above, a bluish gray ; the abdomen yellow ; the whole of the tail of the same colour with the head.

Received from Tranquebar.

OBSERVATIONS.

Though this serpent has no venomous organs, its bite is represented by the natives as infallibly mortal, if proper remedies are not instantly applied.

The present, and the two subjects immediately following, as well as the last five subjects in the First Part of the present Collection, properly belong to the new genus *Hydrus*, some years ago instituted by Mr. Schneider,[*] and adopted by late naturalists. I have, however, though approving of the new genus, adhered to the Linnean classification, for the sake of uniformity ; reserving the alteration for an intended classical index.

The genus Hydrus is thus defined by Mr. Schneider, " Corpus anterius gracile, " sensim crassescens, squamosum. Cauda anceps. Body slender in front, gradually " thickening, squamous. Tail (compressed) two-edged."

[*] Schneider, Amphib. Jena, 1799.

PART II.

To this definition the several subjects alluded to above agree in general ; but I do not comprehend how the serpents No. XVII. XX. XXX. and XXXIII. of the Coromandel Collection, came to be placed by Mr. Schneider in the genus Hydrus ; seeing all the four want the characteristic tail, and none of them possess the general habitus. In regard to two of them, No. XX and XXXIII, Dr. Shaw expresses his opinion that they are not very properly stationed in that genus.[*]

No. XII.

ANGUIS.

Squamæ Abdominales 228 ⎱ 266
Squamæ Subcaudales 38 ⎰

Called by the natives *Shiddil.*

The *head* not thicker than the neck, small, short-ovate. The first pair of lamina square, rounded at the corners, and perforated by the nostrils ; the next pair small round ; the centre lamina between the eyes oval ; the lateral cordate ; on each side of the semicordate laminæ are several large scales.

The *mouth* narrow, the jaws of equal length. There are no fangs ; the teeth very small. The *eyes* high and globular. The *nostrils* large, nearly vertical.

The *trunk* cylindrical to near the tail, where it becomes slightly compressed. The *tail* short, flat, and curve. The *scales* on the occiput and part of the neck, smooth, on the body carinated, and being arranged lozen-wise the carina present as many parallel ridges on the trunk and the tail as there are rows of scales. There is little difference in point of size, of the middle abdominal scales and those on other parts.

The *length* one foot and a half, including the tail, which measures only two inches.

The *colour* buff, with broad rings of black, or dark blue, from the neck to the tip of the tail, which is black. Between the rings on the back, but not on the abdomen, faint darkish spots are interspersed.

OBSERVATIONS.

This serpent was also received from Tranquebar, and its bite is held by the natives to be dangerous though not mortal. It produces, as they pretend, a burning heat over the whole body. It certainly has no venomous apparatus.

[*] Zool: Vol. III: p. 569, 570.

No. XIII.

ANGUIS.

Squamæ Abdominales 244 ⎫
Squamæ Subcaudales 34 ⎭ 278

Called by the natives, *Kadell Nagam.*

The *head* very small, hardly thicker than the neck, oblong, cylindrical ; the fore part covered with laminæ, the rest with small, orbicular, contiguous scales. The front lamina round, with a sharp point inserted between the first pair, which are perforated by the nostrils ; the next pair small, round ; the three laminæ between the eyes nearly of a size, the middle one ovate, accuminated ; the semicordate pair narrow with a broad scale on each side at the point.

The *mouth* small, the upper jaw longer than the under. There are no fangs. The *teeth* minute. The *eyes* globular, and very small. The *nostrils* vertical.

The *trunk.* The neck enormously slender and long, covered above with small orbicular scales ; but underneath there is a series of about forty or fifty scales somewhat larger ; those which succeed are of the same size with the other scales. From the long neck, the body swells and lessens proportionably, but is more compressed as it approaches the tail, which is short, flat, and two edged.

The *length* two feet nine inches ; of which three inches belong to the tail.

The *colour* light blue, with cross yellow bands, more especially on the neck and the tail ; the belly of a lighter yellow, with faint blue bands.

Received from Tranquebar.

OBSERVATIONS.

The bite of this serpent is reputed by the natives to be not less dangerous than that of the Cobra de Capello ; but the absence of poisonous organs sufficiently shows the notion to be a popular error.

It is remarked by the Rev. Mr. John, to whom I am obliged for the present and the two preceding specimens, that he never found a land, a river, or a tank snake with a flat tail. Such as are sometimes found in rivers, have been brought in by the tide, and can live only a short while out of salt water. He remarks further, that it is very difficult to procure sea snakes ; for though often caught in the nets, they are held in such dread by the fishermen that hardly any inducement can procure their preservation : they are first bruised on the head with a billet, and then returned into the water. The Moolagoo Pam (Talla Pam, No XLIV. Corom. Serp.) he says, is often cast on shore by the surf, but rarely any other of the flat tailed snakes.

No. XIV.

COLUBER.

Scuta Abdominalia 144⎫226
Squamæ Subcaudales 82⎭

Called by the natives at Bombay, *Ourdia.*

at Calcutta, *Dora.*

The *head* oblong-ovate, somewhat thicker than the neck, and compressed towards the nose, the fore part covered by nine laminæ. The first pair separating the nostrils small, pyramidal ; the next large, square, rounded behind ; the central lamina between the eyes long, and rather narrow, those on the side conical, convex ; the semicordate pair ample, with several large, smooth scales, on each side. The occiput covered with small orbicular scales.

The *mouth* proportionably small ; there are no fangs ; the marginal row above, as well as all the other teeth, remarkably short. The *eyes* globular. The *nostrils* very small.

The *trunk* swells and diminishes moderately ; but the tail tapers to a fine point. The scales on the neck and on part of the tail smooth ; on the back and sides ovate and carinated ; a row of broader, smooth scales, next to the scuta.

The *length* three feet seven inches ; of which the tail measures eleven inches.

The *colour* of the head light chesnut ; from each orbit proceed two remarkable bluish-black streaks, of unequal length ; the shorter descends obliquely to the mouth the other creeping obliquely along the cheek and the occiput, makes a turn upward to be united with a spot of the same colour on the neck. The back and the sides are also of a bluish-black colour, with dusky-yellow patches every where interspersed. The belly and underpart of the tail are of a yellowish white.

OBSERVATIONS.

The subject described was received from Bombay. Specimens of various sizes have been since received from the same place, as well as from sundry other parts, but without the country names. They varied in colour, being more or less dark, and in the spots being more or less yellow or white ; but the streaks from each orbit were conspicuous in all of them.

It would seem that this species is common. In the different stages of its growth, as well as at different places, it has obtained distinct names ; circumstances in which it is not singular : but the variation in colour in young and old subjects is rather more than usual ; for which reason I have in the following plate given the figures of two of smaller size.

No. XV.

COLUBER A.

Scuta Abdominalia 146 ⎫
Squamæ Subcaudales 82 ⎭ 228

Called by the natives at Tranquebar, *Neer Pamboo*.
at Calcutta, *Dooblee*.
at Bombay,

The *length* one foot two inches and a half, of which the tail measures three inches three-fourths.

The *colour* a dusky lead, with numerous black dots on the back and the sides. The abdomen and under part of the tail white.

COLUBER B.

Scuta Abdominalia 143 ⎫
Squamæ Subcaudales 83 ⎭ 226

Called by the natives at Tranquebar, *Neer Pamboo*.
at Bombay,

The *length* one foot two inches, of which the tail measures three inches four lines.

The *colour* here is less dark, and more spots of dusky yellow are interspersed than in the last subject. Besides the two black lines from each orbit, two specks on the semicordate laminæ are found in both the above subjects, as in all of the same size which I have seen ; but not always in larger subjects.

It were superfluous to enter into a more detailed description, after that given of the *Ourdia*, to which species both certainly belong.

OBSERVATIONS.

Under the name Neer Pamboo, two other serpents, very different from the *Ourdia*, have been received from Tranquebar.

The one, the *Karoo Bokadam*, No. XVII. Coromandel Serpents.

The other *Chittee*. Continuation of Indian Serpents, No. IV.

PART II.

The tail, in this species, would seem to be peculiarly liable to injury. In subjects of a foot in length, it is hardly at the tip thicker than a hair; and in a dozen of specimens of various sizes, the tail was generally found not entire: a circumstance I the rather notice, as it may obviate error in reckoning the subcaudal squamæ.

No. XVI.

BOA.

Scuta Abdominalia   189
Scuta Subcaudalia   18
Squamæ Subcaudales
Boa Johnii.
Called by the natives *Erutaley Nagam.*

The *head* small, round, short, obtuse; covered with small, round, contiguous scales, except on the declivous front, where three pair of small laminæ may be remarked. The first thick and trigonal; the next between the nostrils square; the third pair oblong, and placed obliquely; the common scales between the eyes a little bigger than those on the crown and the occiput.

The *mouth* small and narrow, the upper jaw projecting beyond the under. There are no fangs; the teeth above slender and short, but in front of the under jaw somewhat longer. The *eyes* small, globular, placed near the crown. The *nostrils* high, separated by the second pair of laminæ.

The *trunk* round, for the most part nearly of equal thickness, or swelling a little till within three inches of the vent, where it is thickest, but soon resumes its former size, which it maintains, hardly tapering, to the end of the tail. The obtuse point of the tail resembles the head, and in point of thickness sometimes exceeds it. The scales mostly small, orbicular, smooth, in some places contiguous, mostly imbricated. On each side of the scuta, there is a double row of scales, larger than the dorsal. The scuta broad, and with little diminution in size, are continued on the short tail till within an inch of the point, where they are succeeded by ordinary round scales.

The *length* two feet six inches; of which three inches belong to the tail.

The *colour.* The head, back, and upper part of the tail of an uniform darkish brown; the abdomen of a much paler brown, with more of a reddish cast.

OBSERVATIONS.

The figure was drawn exactly from the specimen received ; but from the stricture and distortion of the subcaudal squamæ, where the scuta terminate, I was led to suspect that the nipple-form end of the tail was an accidental deformity. The suspicion has since been confirmed by two different drawings made in India, and I choose therefore to refer to No. XVII. (a small specimen of the same species) for a more correct representation of the tail, which from the resemblance of its point to the head, has obtained for the serpent the name of double-headed.

Captain Hardwick (lately arrived from Bengal), among many excellent drawings, has got one of this serpent ; and his written description, in the number of subcaudal scuta, agrees exactly with mine. In the small specimen, however, (No. XVII.) the scuta amount to twenty-eight.

The specimen was received from the Rev. Mr. John, of Tranquebar ; but the serpent is not uncommon in Bengal. In the former place, its bite is said to produce leprosy ; an effect often ascribed, by the natives, to many other serpents which have no poisonous organs ; at the latter, it is with more justice deemed perfectly harmless.

Mr. John preserved one of three feet, for more than a twelvemonth, in an earthen pot filled with earth, which was changed once a month. " During the whole time, he " gave it no food ; and except that the thick tail was somewhat extenuated, the animal " suffered no apparent alteration. In its movements it was very slow ; it generally lay " coiled up sluggishly with its head under the belly, was not easily roused, and never " showed a disposition to bite."

It may be remarked, that in the Linnean system, subcaudal squamæ constitute a generic character of Coluber, in like manner as subcaudal scuta do of Boa ; " but " in some few species of Colubri, exclusive of the usual subcaudal scales, are a few " scuta, or undivided lamellæ, either at the beginning or towards the tip of the tail."[*] Of this anomaly, two instances (No. XXXIX. and XL.) occur in the Coromandel collection.

The general habit of the present subject is that of Anguis ; but the unusual breadth of the abdominal as well as subcaudal scuta, and the number of the latter in proportion to the scales on the under surface of the tail, seem to exclude it from that genus. I have therefore classed it with the Boæ, and named it after the respectable missionary who sent me the specimens, to whom I lie under obligation for many communications.

[*] Shaw's Zool. Vol. III. p. 364.

No. XVII.

BOA.

Scuta Abdominalia 193
Scuta Subcaudalia 28
Squamæ Subcaudales
Called by the natives *Manedulli Pamboo.*

This small serpent, though distinguished by a different name, is merely a young subject of the species last described.

The *length* nine inches four lines ; of which the tail claims one inch two lines.

The *colour* a coral red, with irregular black spots and patches on the sides, from the neck to the end of the tail.

The present subject differs from the last in colour, in the number of subcaudal scuta, and in the shape of the tail. In this last respect I consider the present figure more correct, for reasons already assigned.

OBSERVATIONS.

The colour of the figure was copied from an Indian drawing coloured from life ; in the preserved specimen it had faded to a dusky white ; while the spots on the back and the tail, though changed to a pale brown, remained distinctly visible.

No. XVIII.

COLUBER.

Scuta Abdomnalia 191
Squamæ Subcaudales 136 } 327
Called by the natives *Sarey Pamboo.*

The *head* thicker and broader than the neck, oblong, obtuse, flattened on the sides. The first pair of laminæ, which separate the nostrils, are round ; the next pair of the same shape, but twice as large ; the three between the eyes, broad ; the semicordate pair irregularly shaped, and truncate.

The *mouth* wide. A complete marginal row of teeth above : no fangs. The *eyes* large and globular. The *nostrils* ringent.

The *trunk* round, compressed, remarkably slender. The tail long, and tapers to a very slender, round point.

The *length* one foot nine inches and a half, of which the tail claims five inches and a half.

The *colour.* The head cinerious above, and the white cheeks remarkably streaked with black; the neck lead colour, striped with obscure, oblique, black and white lines; but from the middle of the body to the tip of the tail, the colour is more of a bluish gray, and the black stripes more strongly marked. The scuta white, many of them with black margins ; the subcaudal squamæ are still more remarkably checkered black and white.

OBSERVATIONS.

This serpent is not reputed dangerous by the natives ; they nevertheless assert that its bite occasions blindness in persons aged above forty: which I consider as fabulous.

It was received from Tranquebar at the same time with the head of a large one of the same species, which measured in all six feet. The large one was considered by the Rev. Mr. John to be the Jeri Potoo No. XXXIV. of the Coromandel Collection.

He remarks further, that it is often found in company with the Cobra de Capello , and that from the sharpness of its scales it sometimes does harm to the rice grounds.

If I am not mistaken, on a superficial view, small specimens of this serpent are not rare in the English collections.

Where so remarkable a difference of colour between young and old subjects of the same species occurs, as in the foregoing instances No. XV. A, B, XVII. and XVIII. they come naturally to be regarded as distinct species, and different names are conferred on them accordingly. Hence the number in lists of serpents procured from the natives of India, far exceeds the number of existing species ; the same individual in its progressive states obtaining distinct names, the species in consequence come to be fallaciously multiplied.

But however properly the naturalist may, on examination, lessen the number of species, by bringing classically together individuals before separated, yet, to all practical purposes in the country, it must ever be of material consequence (at least in respect to poisonous serpents), to collect not only the provincial names, where different languages obtain, but also the local names in the same dialect applied to different stages of the serpent's growth: for the bite of venomous serpents of every age is always in some degree noxious. The bite of a young Cobra de Capello, though not more than nine inches in length, has been known to prove fatal to a chicken in a few minutes.

PART II.

No. XIX.

COLUBER.

Scuta Abdominalia 271 ⎫
Squamæ Subcaudales 24 ⎬ 295
                        ⎭

Ataligato Seba Thes. V. ii. Tab. 77. fig. 6.

Called by the natives

The *head* small, not thicker than the neck, oblong, round, obtuse, the crown rather flat. The laminæ which separate the nostrils, triangular; the next pair of a roundish shape, and twice as large; the shield-from lamina trigonal and proportionally large, the lateral very small, forming one of several scales which border the orbit; the semi-cordate pair unusually large, and intersected by the point of the shield-form lamina.

The *mouth* narrow. A fang of moderate size on each side, but no marginal row of teeth above. The *eyes* globular, and very small. The *nostrils* on the edge of the rostrum large and open.

The *trunk* cylindrical, somewhat thicker than a swan quill; a little thicker at the middle, and from an inch and a half above the vent diminishes very gradually to the tip of the short tail. The *scales* universally smooth, glistening, as if highly varnished. Those on the neck suborbicular, and rather contiguous than imbricated: on the back the scales are imbricated, and more of an ovate shape.

The *length* thirteen inches eight lines, of which the tail claims nearly one inch.

The *colour* chesnut: the scuta a dull yellow. A narrow, oblique, yellow streak from each nostril, first edges the shield-form lamina, then runs united to the nap of the neck, where it is crossed by a similar line from a yellow patch on each cheek. From the junction of these yellow lines, a chain of white scales runs straight along the middle of the back to the end of the tail, and a similar white thread runs along the side parallel to one of a chesnut colour next to the scuta. The scuta are crossed at unequal distances by narrow dark bands. The white and chesnut threads terminate at the vent; and there are no cross bands on the under part of the tail.

OBSERVATIONS.

I have hardly met with a venomous serpent of less suspicious external appearance than the present subject. The head is covered with regular laminæ, the scales are smooth, close, and varnished, and its body variegated with elegant simplicity; at the same time, it is so peculiarly marked as not to be easily mistaken.

It was received from Java in 1801, without any accompanying history or country name. It is indisputably noxious, though in what degree, or whether it grows to a larger size, are circumstances remaining to be ascertained hereafter.

The description and figure of the *Ataligato* given by Seba suit the present subject so exactly, as to admit little doubt of its being of the identical species. Seba indeed mentions it as a rare Mexican serpent;[*] but several other serpents, besides the Cobra de Capello, are found in the new as well as in the old Continent, or in their respective islands.

It is thus described by Seba " Pulcherrimus hic anguiculus squamis purpureis tenui-
" bus per corpus supernum obsitus. Juxta dorsum protensas gerit tres albicantes
" fasciolas. Venter albus annulis quasi nigris distinguitur. Perpusillum est ejus capi-
" tulum ; et cætera quoque longus et tenuis, rotundulus tamen et glaber conspicitur."

No. XX.

COLUBER.

Scuta Abdominalia   164 ⎫
                              ⎬ 241
Squamæ Subcaudales   77 ⎭

Called by the natives in Java
at Vizagapatam, *Boodro Pam.*

The *head* broader than the neck, swelling out behind on each side, depressed in front, and compressed on the sides of the obtuse rostrum. Close behind the trigonal lamina, which separates the nostrils, a pair of small oval laminæ is placed obliquely ; the scales on the crown smooth, the rest of the head covered with small, orbicular, carinated scales : a narrow lamina above each orbit excepted.

Between the nostril and the eye, on each side, but more on a line with the eye than the nostril, an aperture is observable (similar to that found in the rattle snake) which is larger and more ringent than the nostril.

The *mouth* large. No marginal row of teeth above ; but a long fang on each side, and two remarkably long holders in front of the under jaw. The *eyes* large, globular. The *nostrils* on the verge of the rostrum, very small.

The *trunk* round, slightly compressed ; the *scales* ovate, carinated, imbricate ; but two rows next the scuta on each side larger than the others, hexangular, and smooth. The slender round tail terminates in a fine sharp point.

The *length* one foot eleven inches, of which four inches five lines belong to the tail.

[*] Seba Thes. II. T. 77. f. 6.

The *colour* of the upper half a dark green, which brightening towards the tail, assumes a bluish cast ; the scuta are of a yellowish green, with a bright yellow fillet on each side of the abdomen, continued down half the tail.

OBSERVATIONS.

This serpent was received from Java,, in 1801, together with a large *Bodroo Pam,* and several other serpents more common on the Coromandel coast.

The present subject seems merely a variety of the Bodroo Pam, No. IX. of the Coromandel Collection ; from which it varies principally in the number of subcaudal squamæ, and in the sharp, fine point of the tail.

It was in describing this specimen that I discovered a material mistake committed in my former description of the *Bodroo Pam,* in which the nostrils are represented as " wide and large, and situated near the eyes:"* while the real nostrils, situated near the point of the nose, from their smallness in the recent subject, happened to escape my notice.

This wide aperture near the eyes is similar to that found in the rattle snake, with which I was not then acquainted ; and which I believe had not at that time been remarked in any of the genus Coluber, except in the yellow snake of Martinico.

To the description of the Martinico serpent by Cepede, I owe my escape from a second error, that of attributing double nostrils to the present subject ; and by his remark on the singularity of the aperture, I was led, in conjunction with my friend Mr. Everard Home, to an enquiry, of which the result has lately been communicated to the Royal Society.+

No. XXI.

COLUBER.

$$\left.\begin{array}{ll} \textit{Scuta Abdominalia} & 150 \\ \textit{Squamæ Subcaudales} & 51 \end{array}\right\} 201$$

Called by the natives

The *head* cordate, considerably broader than the neck, depressed ; the rostrum, which is rather pointed than obtuse, compressed near the point. The anterior pair of laminæ small, trigonal ; the next, twice as large, but round ; the shield-form lamina well shaped, the lateral truncate cones slightly convex ; the simicordate pair broad and short : small, orbicular, contiguous scales cover the occiput.

* Coromandel Serpents, No. IX.   + Phil. Transact. 1804. Part I. p. 70.

Between the rostrum and the eye, situated as in the Bodroo Pam, there is a ringent aperture on each side, considerably larger than the nostril. The *mouth* wide. The fangs visible one each side, remarkably long. No marginal row above, and the palatal row, as well as the teeth in the under jaw, unusually small. The *eyes* globular. The *nostrils* very small, placed at the base of the front lamina. The *trunk*. From the head to the end of the tail carinated, the sides, which at first are compressed, dilate as they approach the flat, or plain abdomen. The *tail* taper rapidly to a small sharp point. The *scales* ovate, smooth, imbricate. The *length* twelve inches and a half: the tail two inches two lines. The *colour*. The upper part of the head brown, with a cineritious fillet on both sides running obliquely from each orbit along the occiput. The general colour cineritious, with many round or oval dark spots, of which thirty-three pair may be counted from the hind head to the end of the tail: some of the spots have ragged edges, and each pair nearly joins at the dorsal carina. The white abdomen is strewed with dusky dots and short lines: and next to the scuta on each side there is a row of small, dusky, round spots, which grow fainter and fainter as they approach the tail.

OBSERVATIONS.

This serpent also was received from Java, without name or memoranda relative to its history.

It affords another instance of a venomous serpent with large laminæ on the head, and scales on the trunk not carinated. Of the former, Cepede had met with no example except in the Coluber Naja. "Je n'ai vu que sur la tête du Naja les neuf grandes écailles "qui garnissent celle de la plupart du Couleuvres ovipares et non venimeuses." *
Considering the number of serpents Cepede examined, this remark deserves particular notice. He afterwards, however, found a second instance in the Coluber Hemachate;+ and Shaw gives a third in the Coluber Porphyriacus from New Holland. ‡

* Hist. Natur. V. II. Discours. p. 67, 88.   + P. 115.   ‡ Zool. V. III. p. 423.

PART II.

No. XXII.

COLUBER.

Scuta Abdominalia   151 ⎫
                          ⎬ 197
Squamæ Subcaudales   46 ⎭

Called by the natives

The *head* big, thicker than the neck, ovate, slightly depressed, the rostrum compressed on the sides, and the point turning up. Between the nose and shield-form lamina, small, smooth, orbicular scales surround a pair of round laminæ; of the three between the eyes the middle lamina is narrow, lance-shape; the lateral broad and convex; the semicordate pair short: the occiput covered with smooth orbicular scales, smaller than those in front.

The ringent aperture between the nostril and the eye is also found here, in the same situation as in the two preceding subjects.

The *mouth* rather large. There are fangs on each side, of a size proportionably large: no marginal teeth above, and the palatal teeth in the under jaw small. The *eyes* oval, large. The *nostrils*, near the point of the reverted rostrum, very small.

The *trunk*. The neck slender; the body towards the middle rather thick; the back carinated, the sides swelling to the abdomen, which is convex, not flat as in the last. The *tail* terminates in a small horny point. The *scales* on the back carinated, but smooth on other parts.

The *length* one foot two inches and a half, including the tail of two inches and a half.

The *colour*. The upper part of the head dark brown, with a cineritious streak from each orbit. The trunk of a lighter brown than the head, with cinerious and brown oval spots on the back and sides. The belly yellowish, freckled with minute dots. On each side of the fore part of the trunk, there is a row of small darkish spots next the scuta.

OBSERVATIONS.

This serpent was received from India in 1802 without country name, or the place where it was found being specified.

It has more of the viper appearance than the last. The dorsal scales are carinated, and the laminæ on the head less regular than usual: yet, except on the rostrum, they are more completely formed than commonly found in venomous serpents.

" Quelques serpens venimeux (says Cepede) ont quelquefois entre les yeux trois
" écailles un peu plus grandes que celles du dos."° This peculiarity, however, does
not apply to the laminæ in the present subject.

In the observations on the Bodroo Pam (No. XX.), reference was made to a paper
lately published in the Philosophical Transactions, " on the Orifices found in certain
" venomous Snakes situated between the nostril and the eye:" of which the three
subjects immediately preceding afford examples.

Similar orifices in the rattle snake had long since been described, and were sus-
pected of being the external organs of hearing ;+ but were regarded as peculiar to the
Crotalus, and had not been found, so far as I know, in any of the other serpent tribe,
till discovered in the yellow snake of Martinico.

On a cursory inspection of several collections in London, these orifices were
found in three of the genus Boa; and in eleven of the genus Coluber; exclusively of
the Martinico snake, the Bodroo Pam, the two subjects last described, and two others
lately received from the West Indies. In all, three Boæ, and fifteen or sixteen
Colubri.

Hitherto the orifices have only been found in venomous serpents; but in none of
the genus Anguis.

It being intended, in a subsequent fasciculus, to give the figures explanatory of Mr.
Home's anatomical investigation, it will be sufficient to remark here, his having
clearly ascertained that the orifice near the eye in these venomous serpents, has no
connexion whatever with the auditory organ.

No. XXIII.

COLUBER.

Scuta Abdominalia   210 ⎫
Squamæ Subcaudales   93 ⎬303
Called by the natives

The *head* small, short-ovate, obtuse, covered with nine laminæ. The first pair
between the nostrils, rounded in front ; the next pair square and larger ; the middle
lamina between the eyes heart-shape, the lateral semilunate; the semicordate pair long
and obtuse.

The *mouth* large ; the teeth small ; no fangs. The *eyes* large and globular. The
nostrils wide.

° Hist. Nat. V. II. Discours. p. 67.   + Phil. Transact. Vol. XIII. p. 26.

The *trunk.* The neck roundish, smaller than the head. The body much compressed, and more slender near the vent than near the head. The *tail* tapers rapidly to a long, small, horny point. The *scales* ovate, and smooth.

The *length* two feet three inches, of which five inches belong to the tail.

The *colour.* The head cineritious, with an oblique black fillet from each orbit; and a bifid blotch of the same colour on the crown: the cheeks streaked with black. The trunk nearly of the colour of the head, with a row of distinct dark brown spots, round or oval, on each side of the ridge of the back: on the tail, the spots run into each other. The scuta are marked on their anterior edges, with four, or three, obsolete dusky points.

OBSERVATIONS.

The specimen was received from Java, without country name, or description. Of four different specimens examined, the variation in the number of scuta and squamæ was very inconsiderable: the colour and maculæ were alike in all.

The present subject, in the compressed form of the trunk, in the colour and disposition of the dorsal spots, bears a strong resemblance to the serpent last described.

No. XXIV.

COLUBER.

Scuta Abdominalia   209 ⎫
Squamæ Subcaudales 160 ⎭ 369

Serpens viridis ore acuminato Aspidis species.   Seba
Thes. V. ii. Tab. 57. fig. 4.

Col. Nasutus. Shaw Zool. V. iii. Part ii. p. 548.

Called by the natives

The *head* long, wedge-form; the rostrum narrow, compressed, sharp, but not turned up at the point as in the Coluber Mycterizans. The usual front lamina (which in other serpents covers the point of the nose) extends internally on the mouth, and projects externally a very little beyond the first pair of laminæ. In the Coluber Mycterizans, the front lamina though somewhat reverted interiorly, is elongated externally into a slender blunt point which turns upwards and backwards: in other respects there is a strong similitude. The first pair of laminæ separating the nostrils, pyramidal, cut obliquely at the base; the next pair oblong, large, rounded behind; the central lamina of the three between the eyes, funnel-shape ; the lateral, projecting over the eyes, broad, pyramidal ; the semi-cordate regularly formed.

The *mouth* rather wide ; there are no fangs ; but a complete marginal row of teeth above. The *eyes* oval, large, lateral, placed in grooves, which extend to the nostrils. The *nostrils* very small, and distant from each other.

The *trunk*, thicker in all its proportions than that of the Coluber Mycterizans, but *tail* long, slender, and taper to a sharp point. The *scales* smooth, linear or oblong on the upper part of the trunk, though rather tending more to oval than in the Coluber Mycterizans, or the Bolla Passerchi formerly described.*

The *length*, four feet eleven inches, of which the tail measures one foot eight.

The *colour* green as in the Coluber Mycterizans, and a yellow thread runs also along each side of the scuta, and subcaudal squamæ, from the throat to the end of the tail.

OBSERVATIONS.

This subject was received from Java, and I had no doubt of its being the green serpent found in Seba, to which I have referred.

Its similitude to the Coluber Mycterizans is striking at first sight ; but besides its general habitude, the straight pointed rostrum sufficiently distinguishes it.

No. XXV.

COLUBER.

Scuta Abdominalia   186.
Squamæ Subcaudales   153.
Called by the natives, *Mancas* in Guzerat.
Rooka in Mahratta.

The *head* somewhat broader than the neck, oblong, flattened on the crown, and also on the sides from the eyes to the obtuse or rounded rostrum. Two square laminæ divide the nostrils ; the next pair larger, of the same shape ; the middle lamina between the eyes funnel-shaped ; those on the side large ; the semicordate pair regularly shaped, with some large scales on each side of the point.

The *mouth* large. Two rows of teeth above ; no fangs. The *eyes* oval and remarkably large. The *nostrils* rather large.

The *trunk* cylindrical, elegantly shaped. A remarkable series of oblong-round scales on the ridge of the back, and a row of pentagonal scales on each side of the scuta ; the

* Coromandel Serpents, No. XIII.

other scales linear disposed in oblique rows. The *tail* tapers to a slender point, and
is covered with scales nearly orbicular.

The *length* three feet five inches, of which one foot two belongs to the tail.

The *gull*, when biggest, one inch and a half.

The *colour* of the upper part of the head and trunk dark blue ; the neck, abdomen,
and tail, a bluish white. The colour in the recent subject is probably more green.

OBSERVATIONS.

The laminæ of the head in this serpent, as well as the disposition of the linear scales
on the trunk, resemble those of the Coluber Mycterizans, or Passerchi Pam.

The specimen was received from Bombay, sent with several others by Dr. Scott.

It was declared very venomous by our snake-catcher, who said he had known two
men killed by it. By another its bite was said to occasion immediate giddiness, and to
prove mortal in two days.

It is represented as living on trees ; and not uncommon.

No. XXVI.

COLUBER.

Scuta Abdominalia   176.
Squamæ Subcaudales   127.
Called by the natives *Cumberi muken*.

The *head* hardly thicker than the neck, oblong, obtuse. The front pair of laminæ
nearly square, rounded only a little on the posterior edge ; the next pair of the same
shape, but larger in size ; the middle laminæ of the next three behind, funnel-shaped ;
the lateral, broad, conical ; the semicordate pair well shaped, with two little specks, or
dots in the middle.

The *mouth* large. No fangs. A full row of teeth above, and in the under jaw the
teeth are numerous and close.

The *eyes* large, and globular. The *nostrils* large, and situated on the edge of the rostrum.

The *trunk* rather slender in proportion to its length, but cylindrical and well-shaped.
The *tail* attenuates gradually to a sharp point. The *scales* on the neck near the head are
orbicular ; but from that to the vent they are oblong, or linear ; except a row of large
hexagonal scales on the ridge of the back, and a similar series on each side of the scuta.
The linear scales are not continued on the tail, but give place to hexagonal.

The *length* three feet eight, of which the tail measures one foot one inch and a half.

OBSERVATIONS.

The specimen was received from Mr. John of Tranquebar, who represents the serpent as extremely beautiful when alive.

It certainly has no poisonous apparatus, though said by the natives to be highly noxious. They account for its name (implying *top-climber*) in the following manner: that after the death of the person bitten, it ascends a tree near the funeral pile, looking down, as if with malicious pleasure, while the corpse is consuming.

This serpent is described by Schneider.* He mentions two specimens in Block's Museum. In one, Scuta 198, Squamæ 158; in the other, Scuta 144, Squamæ 65

In two drawings received from Mr. John the Scuta are 190, Squamæ 150.

The difference in the subcaudal squamæ in Schneider's description, may possibly be owing to the tail having been mutilated, a common accident, where it is so slender near the point, as in the Coluber Mycterizans and others; the difference in the scuta, supposing no error in counting, is greater than I ever met with in the same species, being no less than 65.

He describes the scales as carinated, which I found smooth.

No. XXVII.

ANGUIS.

Squamæ Abdominales 206
Squamæ Subcaudales 8.
Anguis Scytale Lin. Sys. Nat. p. 923. Called by the natives

The *head*, small, short, a little more depressed and obtuse than the tail, to which it bears a resemblance sufficient to entitle it to the denomination of double-headed snake. The front trigonal lamina intersects two of the same shape, which are perforated by the nostrils; the next pair large irregularly square; behind, five trigonal laminæ occupy the place of the shield-form, lateral, and semicordate.

The *mouth* wide, the lower jaw shorter than the upper. A marginal row of teeth above; no fangs. The *eyes* globular, very small. The *nostrils* small also.

The *trunk* cylindrical, swells a little to the middle, and afterwards diminishes very gradually, so that the short tail is nearly as big as the head but less obtuse. The *scales* orbicular, polished, and ciliated; contiguous in some places, in others imbricate, and

* Hist. Amph. Java, II. p. 299.

so disposed as to appear polygonal. A series consisting of about 206 may be counted on the middle of the abdomen, hardly, if any thing, larger than the dorsal scales; but the subcaudal squamæ are very different, and might be termed scuta. The *tail* is very short, thick, cordate.

The *length*, one foot eight inches, of which the tail claims only half an inch. The circumferences of the neck one inch and a half; middle of the trunk two inches; near the vent one inch seven lines.

The *colour* of the head and back bluish black; two yellowish spots on the nose, and two or three incomplete rings of the same colour on the occiput and neck. The belly of the same colour with the back and sides, but crossed by more than 30 broad, yellowish rings with ragged edges, some complete, but most of them imperfect; the under part of the tail yellow tipped with black, and a black dot on each side of the vent.

OBSERVATIONS.

This anguis was received from Java, without description, or local name.

Though it agrees in several circumstances with the Anguis Scytale of Linneus, it differs materially in the number of squamæ. The dilatation of the subcaudal squamæ resembling scuta is not marked in any of the descriptions or figures of the Scytale which have fallen in my way.

No. XXVIII.

ANGUIS.

Squamæ Abdominales 207.
Squamæ Subcaudales 6.
Called by the natives *Shilay Pamboo.*

The *head* of this serpent thicker and more depressed than the very short thick tail, which, with a black dot on each side resembling eyes, might at first sight be mistaken for the head. The anterior pair of laminæ are trigonal, and perforated near the base by the nostrils; the second pair large, oblong; between the eyes are three trigonal laminæ, indented; behind which there is a cluster of smaller angular laminæ.

The *mouth* proportionably large. A marginal row of teeth above; no fangs. The *eyes* orbicular, very small. The *nostrils* on the edge of the rostrum.

The *trunk* cylindrical, not much thicker than a swan's quill, and nearly of equal thickness throughout. The *tail* short, ovate, smaller than the head, and ends in a blunt point. The *scales* on the occiput and upper part of the neck, round and contiguous; on other parts more ovate and imbricate. They are all smooth, and look as if varnished; there is no abdominal row distinguished by their size; but the subcaudal squamæ resemble scutella.

The *length* nine inches, two lines; the latter claimed by the tail.

The *colour* on the crown and back dark chesnut; there is a narrow, cross, yellowish fillet on the occiput, and two of the same colour on the neck; along the rest of the trunk may be counted about twenty-eight pair of similar fillets, these points alternating, not joining; the abdomen of a lighter chesnut, with above thirty cross bands of paler brown with ragged margins; the under part of the tail lighter than the abdomen, and on each side of the vent there is a black dot.

OBSERVATIONS.

Two specimens of this serpent were received from Tranquebar, where its bite is said to produce great weakness, and such a wasting of flesh, that the skin hangs loose, and may be handled like a piece of white cloth. The absence of poisonous organs stands against this fiction.

No. XXIX.

ANGUIS.

Squamæ Abdominales 194.
Squamæ Subcaudales 6.
Anguis Maculata; Lin. Sys. Nat. 391. Called by the natives

The *head* not thicker than the neck, short; the front slightly declivous, the rostrum obtuse. The front pair of laminæ triangular, and perforated by the nostrils; the next pair large, sub-orbicular; the three between the eyes ovate, the middle one smallest; in the place of the semicordate laminæ there are two ovate, and scales of the same shape cover the occiput.

The *mouth* rather wide, the marginal row of teeth complete: no fangs. The *eyes* orbicular, distant, small. The *nostrils* small.

The *trunk* is sub-cylindrical, and nearly of equal thickness, or swells very inconsiderably; the circumference within an inch of the vent rather exceeds that of the neck, and the short tail differs less from the head in size than in shape.

PART III.

The *scales* near the head contiguous; on other parts imbricated : but all sub-orbicular, smooth, ciliated, splendent, and differ little in size. The subcaudal scutella, as in the two former subjects, are found here also, though in one specimen less expanded.

The *length* ten inches, of which half an inch belongs to the tail.

The *colour.* The head blackish, with two yellowish devaricating streaks from the crown, and two roundish spots of the same colour on the neck. The trunk above presents thirty-six pair of reddish-brown sub-orbicular spots of various sizes, with black margins of various breadths, an undulating black thread that runs along the ridge of the back serving as part of the margin to each pair. The yellowish-white abdomen is crossed by twenty-eight bands, broader, but of the same colour as the margins above, with which they are united ; in some places the belly appears tesselated black and white.

OBSERVATIONS.

This anguis was received from India without the country name, or mention from whence sent.

There can be no doubt of this being the Anguis Maculata of Linnæus, but it is remarkable that the difference in subcaudal squamæ as given by Gronovius (no less than five) should not have been noticed by Linnæus, who cites Gronovius ; and that the dilatation of the subcaudal squamæ, as a deviation from the generic character, should have passed unnoticed by Linnæus in his own description.*

It should however be remarked that of two specimens, the expansion of squamæ in one was less perceptible than in the other from which the drawing was made.

No. XXX.

COLUBER.

Scuta Abdominalia 220 ⎫
                         ⎬ 281.
Squamæ Subcaudales 61 ⎭

Called by the natives *Chunalee.*

The *head* broader than the neck, long oval, depressed above ; the rostrum compressed, obtuse. Between the nostrils are interposed two pentagonal laminæ; the next pair larger, sub-triangular ; behind which appear an unusual row of small laminæ ; the shield-form laminæ exactly shaped, those on each side convex, sub-lunated ; the semi-

* Mus. Ad. Ic. p. 31.

cordate pair truncate, obscurely divided, and marked with four darkish dots ; the hind head covered with smooth orbicular scales.

The *mouth* large ; the under jaw considerably shorter than the upper. The *teeth* remarkably small ; a marginal row above, and no fangs. The *eyes* large, sub-orbicular. The *nostrils* small.

The *trunk.* The *neck,* at first smaller than the head, swells into the trunk, which is well and proportionally formed : the *tail* round, remarkably short, terminates in a slender point. The scales oval, smooth, and every where very small in size ; and the usual row of larger scales bordering the scuta is wanting. The scuta remarkably wide.

The *length,* three feet four inches, of which the tail measures seven inches four lines.

The *colour* above cineritious, with large darkish ragged spots along the ridge of the back, while others smaller and more faint are scattered on the sides. The abdomen and under part of the tail uniformly white without spots.

OBSERVATIONS.

Two specimens in good preservation were received from Dr. Scott, of Bombay, sent to him from Buchier, by Mr. Bruce. The serpent, it seems, is found also in the Mahratta country.

The natives pretend that its bite is in a short while followed by blotches on the skin, and proves mortal in a fortnight, or within the month.

The serpent, however, has no venomous organs.

The smaller of the two specimens is here described. The only difference found was in the abdominal scuta, the number of which in the largest was 238.

$$\begin{array}{r} \text{In the lesser,} \quad 220. \\ \hline 18. \end{array}$$

No. XXXI.

BOA.

Scuta Abdominalia 204.
Scuta Subcaudalia 44.
Called by the natives *Seu Walalay.*

The *head* obtuse ovate, a little thicker than the neck, the crown flat, the rostrum rounded at the point, but flattish on the sides. The first pair of laminæ between the nostrils very small, sub-orbicular ; the next pair thrice as large, oblong-square, anteriorly rounded ; the shield-form lamina broad, and short, the lateral remarkably slender ; the semi-cordate pair large, with several small laminæ on the sides.

The *mouth* moderate in size ; the teeth very slender ; the palatal teeth complete, but no marginal row, the fang on each side extremely small. The *eyes* on the side, distant, globular, small. The *nostrils* small, on the verge of the rostrum, distant from each other.

The *trunk* cylindrical, swelling very moderately, from two inches behind the head to within four inches of the vent ; it then tapers to the tail, which is short, with a small point, but not sharp. The *scales* small, close, imbricate, ovate, but on the ridge of the back to the end of the tail there is a series of somewhat larger, orbicular, or rather hexangular scales ; all are smooth, and splendent.

The *length* two feet three inches, of which the tail measures four inches two lines.

The *colour* of the head and about one third of the upper part of the trunk a pale yellowish brown ; the rest a reddish brown, variegated with rings composed of pale or whitish short lines, rather than dots, intermixed with the brown scales. The abdomen white, with a yellowish cast, without spots.

OBSERVATIONS.

The present subject was received from Mr. John, of Tranquebar, and is clearly a variety of the Gedi Paragoodoo, No. I. of the Coromandel Collection, which by the Tamuls is named Karu Walalay. The present is distinguished on account of its colour, and called Brown Walalay. I never met with it in the Circars, nor with a Gedi Paragoodoo without rings, which Mr. John once saw.

On the subject of the Gedi Paragoodoo, it may be proper to remark here that I have two specimens from Bombay of a size much larger than I met with in the Circars.

The largest,	Scuta Abdom.	220.	Length	3 feet 11 inches.
	Scuta Subcaud.	50.	Tail - -	5 inches 2 lines.
			Circumference -	3 inches and half.
The smallest,	Scuta Abdom.	221.	Length	3 feet 7 inches.
	Scuta Subcaud.	52.	Tail - -	5 inches 5 lines.

Both specimens, except the number of abdominal scuta, agreed exactly with the description formerly given of the Gedi Paragoodoo.

No. XXXII.

COLUBER.

Scuta Abdominalia 170.
Squamæ Subcaudales 54.
Serpens Ceilonica Bitin dicta, Seba, II. t. 94.
Ulpera, Gron. Amph. No. XLII. p. 68.
Coluber Lachesis, Shaw Zool. III. p. 2, 402.

Called by the natives

The *head* somewhat broader than the neck, thick, oblong, contracted at the rostrum ; the crown flattish, and covered with small, ovate, imbricate, and carinated scales. A large, triangular, convex, lamina fronts the compressed rostrum, on each side of which, two smaller edge the nostril. Between the nostrils there is a remarkable rose-fashion cluster of small, smooth, orbicular, contiguous scales or laminæ. The upper edge of the orbit is covered by an oblong thin lamina, as one more lineal does that of the nostril. All the rest of the scales on the head are carinated, except a few on the cheeks smooth, and orbicular.

The *mouth* large ; the teeth in the under jaw, as well as the palatal rows above, remarkably slender ; and the fangs, on each side in the usual situation, were proportionally not large.

The *eyes* oval, rather small. The *nostrils* on the side of the compressed rostrum, large, ringent, and near each other.

The *trunk* roundish, thick, and clumsy. The *tail* short, round, tapering to a horny point, which is covered above with scales. The *scales* long ovate, and highly carinated, except a row on each side of the abdomen, smooth and orbicular. They are all strongly adherent on the anterior part, but towards the point loose and detached, as if capable of ruffling on erection. The scuta remarkably broad.

The *length* four feet six inches, of which the tail measures seven inches 3 lines.

The *colour* a light brown, with large sub-orbicular, chesnut-coloured spots from the neck to the vent. The scuta white ; bordered half way down the trunk, by distant, black dusky spots, three-fourths smaller than those on the back.

REMARKS

This subject, killed at Bombay in 1803, was received from Dr. Scott, and supposed to be of the same species by which a boy, belonging to Mr. Leachman, had been mortally wounded a few years before. From its venemous apparatus no doubt can be entertained of its atrociousness, and indeed all external appearances condemn it.

I have referred to the figure in Seba, Tab. 94, as approaching nearest to the present subject. It differs however in the shape of the rostrum, and still more in representing fangs in the under jaw: an anomaly of which there is no other instance, so far as I know.

That Seba ascribes fangs to both jaws can admit of no doubt. "Ori tam supra, quam infra, haud plures quatuor insident dentes, longi, incurvi, acuti, quos emittere rursus rursusque recondere valet animal." Vol. II. p. 99.

The Serpens Corallina Amboinensis of Seba, Pl. 30, has no fangs in the under jaw, and in the shape and lamina of the rostrum, comes nearer my specimen than either of the figures, Pl. 93 and 94.

What Seba depicts as testiculos, Tab. 93, is the double penis, and in my specimen is much more conspicuous ; so that his Bitin, Pl. 94, is not a female.

A good description of the Bitin, as far as a dried specimen admitted, has been given by Gronovius (Amph. Zool. Hist. Pl. 68, No. XLI.) ; but though he refers, under doubt, to the figures in Seba, it is plain from the shape and shortness of the tail, that his Bitin belonged to neither of the two, but rather to the Serpens Corallina Amboinensis of Seba, Tab. 30. The abdominal scuta in his specimen were 141, the caudal squamæ 24.

Much has been written concerning this serpent ; authors in succession copying from one another. Fernandes (Hist. Rept. Tract. III. p. 70, Rome 15.) represents it of enormous bulk, in the Island of Cuba, with fangs of the length of a finger

No. XXXIII.

COLUBER.

JAVA.

Scutæ 168.
Squamæ 84.

The *head* ovate, obtuse, a little broader than the neck, depressed, covered chiefly with small orbicular smooth scales behind, the laminæ extending only to the crown. The first pair of laminæ large, round, and perforated by the nostrils. Behind these are two triangular, and one diamond shape: all these are black. The next pair roundish. The semicordate very short.

The *mouth* proportional; a complete marginal row (of teeth) above. No fangs. The *eyes* small. The *nostrils* vertical, very minute.

The *trunk* cylindrical, and covered with very small, oval, close (slightly carinated) scales. The *tail* short, tapering to a small obtuse point. The row of scales next the scutæ are not larger than the others. The middle lamina between the eyes, narrow, lance shape; the lateral (ones) broad.

The *length* one foot one inch, of which the *tail* measures three inches.

The *colour* black (or very dark brown), with cross bands of dusky yellow, at equal distances, half surrounding the trunk, from the neck to the end of the tail: a remarkable cowl of the same dusky yellow on the hind head. The scutæ are of a lighter yellow, with a row of distant black spots on each side. The under part of the tail speckled with black.

No. XXXIV.

COLUBER.

JAVA

Scutæ 140.
Squamæ 42.

The *head* hardly thicker than the neck, oblong, ovate. The first pair of laminæ trigonal; and the second, irregularly square, rounded. The shield-form lamina sharp-pointed; the lateral lamina conical, the semi-cordate pair truncate.

The *mouth* small; no fangs; a marginal row of teeth above. The *eyes* not large, orbicular.

The *nostrils* minute, but open.

The *trunk*. The neck and body cylindrical; the latter swelling a little about the middle, tapers towards the tail, which is thick and short, ending in a sharp point.

The *length*, one foot one inch and three lines, of which the tail measures two inches and seven lines.

The *colour* dark chesnut, intermixed on the upper part of the body, with waving whitish dotted lines, forming imperfect squares. The *cheeks* and *rostrum* light, and there is a collar of yellowish white round the neck. Along the centre of the back there are twelve larger white irregular-shaped dots, each surrounded by a black margin. The scutæ yellow: one half of every third or fourth scuta chequered with black.

No. XXXV.

COLUBER.

JAVA.

Scutæ 144.
Squamæ 33; *tail broken.*

The *head* oblong, ovate, a little broader than the neck. The first pair of laminæ trigonal, the second pair larger, and roundish. The shield-form lamina completely regular, the lateral, narrow; the semicordate pair large, with a white speck on each.

The *mouth* rather large, without fangs. The *eyes* large, orbicular. The *nostrils* small, vertical.

The *trunk*. The body swells and tapers inconsiderably; the *tail* round, thick, taper, but had been broken. The *scales* oval, and some rows on the back very slightly carinated.

The *length*, one foot four inches three lines. The broken tail measured three inches two lines.

The *colour*. The head black, or very dark brown. The cheeks streaked with black. The trunk striped. Along the ridge of the back, to the end of the tail, runs a black thread, on each side of which are two parallel broad fillets; the one, a mixed cinereous brown, the other black. The scutæ white, edged with brownish black, giving the appearance of so many cross bands; but on the tail the bands are divided in the middle.

No. XXXVI.

COLUBER NAJA.
JAVA, XVII.

Scutæ 186.
Squamæ 64.

This specimen is of nearly the same size with a specimen received from Tranquebar, *Scutæ* 180,⎫ but the principal difference is in the colour and circular bands on the *Squamæ* 57,⎭ trunk, which I never observed in young subjects on the Coast.

The *length* of this specimen is one foot two inches two lines.

No. XXXVII.

COLUBER.
JAVA, XIII.

Scutæ 194.
Squamæ 66.

The *head* ovate, flat, thin. Two roundish laminæ between the nostrils ; the next pair nearly square; the shield lamina bell-form; the semi-cordate pair obtuse.

The *mouth* of moderate size ; no fangs. A marginal row of teeth above. The *eyes* very small, globular. The *nostrils* minute.

The *trunk* round ; swells and tapers proportionally ; a little compressed about the middle. The *tail* short, with a round point. The *scales* ovate, smooth.

The *length*, one foot seven inches. The *tail*, three inches and three quarters.

The *colour*, dark brown, freckled with dusky, yellow, short, waving threads, which form irregularly oval spots along the back. The *belly*, white.

No. XXXVIII.

COLUBER.

JAVA, XIV.

Scutæ 170.
Squamæ 52.

The *head* obtuse, ovate, scarcely broader than the neck; *rostrum* rounded. On the point of the front laminæ a trigonal pair separates the nostrils; behind these a narrow pair. The shield-form lamina very broad, acuminated; the semi-cordate, well shaped.

The *mouth* without fangs. The *eyes* spherical. The *nostrils* lateral, very small.

The *trunk* is of the thickness of a small goose-quill, tapers to a sharp point at the tail. The *scales* smooth.

The *length*, seven inches three lines, of which the tail measures one inch two lines.

The *colour*. A black double fillet crosses the orbits, and there is an oblique streak of the same colour on each cheek. From the middle of the shield-form lamina rises a black fillet, which, dividing into two, is continued on each side of the ridge of the back to the tip of the tail: two narrower stripes of the like colour run parallel to these as far as the anus. These fillets are edged with very fine white lines. There are two other smaller waving lines on each side, which extend the whole length of the body. The colour between these stripes is a light bay, so that the body appears black and bay alternately. The *belly*, dusky white.

No. XXXIX.

COLUBER.

INDIA, I.

Scutæ 202.
Squamæ 68.

The *head*, oblong, ovate, flat, considerably broader than the neck. The first pair of laminæ rounded; the second pair much larger. The shield-form lanceolate; the semi-cordate pair small, but well shaped.

INDIAN SERPENTS.

The *mouth* large, without fangs ; a marginal row of teeth above.

The *eyes* small, orbicular. The *nostrils* small.

The *trunk*. The body is small for its length, gradually enlarges till beyond the middle ; it then as gradually decreases towards the anus, where it suddenly becomes less, and terminates in a small sharp pointed tail. The *scales* are every where very obtuse.

The *length*, one foot eight inches, of which the tail measures three inches and a half.

The *colour*. The head dark brown, the cheeks striped with the same colour ; the back is of a lighter brown, having a dull greenish tint, which grows fainter at the sides, and is lost as it approaches the scutæ. The *belly* is white.

No. XL.

COLUBER.

INDIA, II.

Scutæ 151.
Squamæ 46.

The *head* small, rostrum obtuse. The first pair of laminæ small, and nearly orbicular, and are perforated by the *nostrils*. The second pair very small, triangular. A third pair a little larger, ovate. These terminate at the orbits of the *eyes:* the remainder of the *head* is covered by very small orbicular scales, which towards the occiput become carinated. The *mouth* small, no fangs, a marginal row of very small *teeth* above. The *nostrils* small. The *eyes* small, ovate.

The *trunk*. The body thick round, and tapers very gradually into the *tail*. The *scales* are long oval, and carinate throughout.

The *tail* is short, and terminates abruptly, appearing as though a small part had been lost by accident during life.

The *length*, one foot eight inches, of which the imperfect tail three inches, two lines.

The *colour*. The upper part of the head, back, and tail, are of an uniform bluish black colour. The sides are uniformly marked from the chin to the extremity of the tail, with rounded spots of the same colour as the back. These spots regularly alternate with each other, and are connected to one another by slips, from a smaller row of irregular shaped spots along the middle of the belly. The *belly*, white.

No. XLI.

COLUBER.
JAVA, XVI.

Scutæ   217. 215.
Squamæ   76. 78.

The *head* broader than the neck, the occiput swelling out. The rostrum obtuse. The lamina between the nostrils small, square; the next pair of the same shape, remarkably large; the three between the eyes remarkably small; the central one resembles the point of a lancet, the lateral, pyramidal, short. The semi-cordate pair long, with several large scales on each side.

The *mouth* proportionally narrow; the *teeth* very small, a marginal row above; no fangs. The *eyes* globular, very small; the *nostrils* large.

The *trunk* cylindrical, swells and lessens moderately; the *tail* tapers more sensibly to a very small not acute point. The *abdomen* flattish; the *scales* remarkably small, ovate, smooth, close.

The *length*, three feet one inch and a half; of which the tail measures seven inches.

The *colour*. The head a yellowish bay; the trunk dark brown, deepening towards the tail; six or eight yellowish bands are visible on the back, narrow on the ridge of the back, and expanding towards the scutæ; they are bright on the neck, but evanescent about the middle of the trunk. The scutæ, and other parts beneath, are of nearly the same colour with the bands; but both may probably have been altered by the spirit.

No. XLII.

COLUBER.
JAVA, XVI.

Scutæ   238.
Squamæ   95.

The *head* very little larger than the neck. The front lamina trigonal; the first pair pentagonal; the second nearly of the same form, but much larger. The shield-form lamina regular ; the lateral ones sub-conical, the semicordate pair broad, obtuse, having a large lamina on each side near their apex.

The *mouth* proportionally large ; a marginal row of teeth above ; no fangs. The *eyes* large ; globular. The *nostrils* close to the rostrum, rounded, open.

The *trunk* depressed ; scales ovate, smooth. The *tail* round, gradually tapering to an obtuse point.

The *length,* three feet eight inches and a half, of which the tail measures nine inches.

The *colour,* a bright bay, inclining to yellow. A black line passes up the cheek to the eye, and from thence back and downwards to the angle of the mouth. Another line runs from the eye, along the margin of the semicordate pair of laminæ, and terminates in a transverse band of black at the occiput. From thence begin fillets, which gradually become wider and blacker, and afterwards diminish in strength, become broken, and finally disappear about half way towards the tail. These fillets have a white dot, or break at every inch distance. On each side, at a small distance from the former, is a much smaller dark line, which is more broken, becomes fainter, and is lost at the same part of the body with the other fillets. The remainder of the body and tail is of a uniform light bay colour, which becomes weaker at the sides. The *belly* is white.

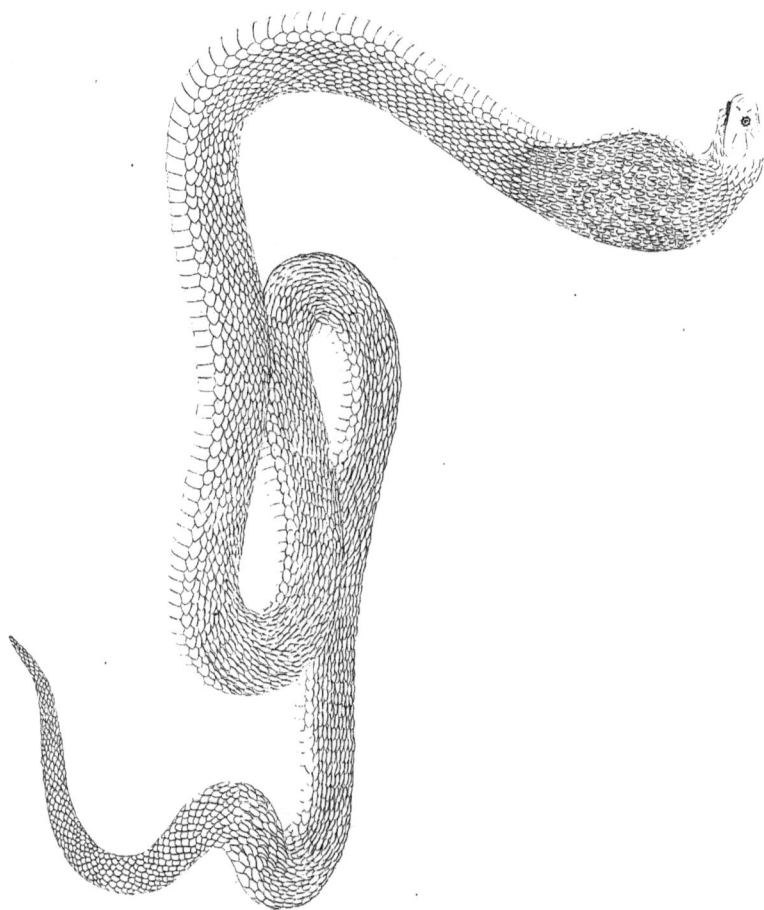

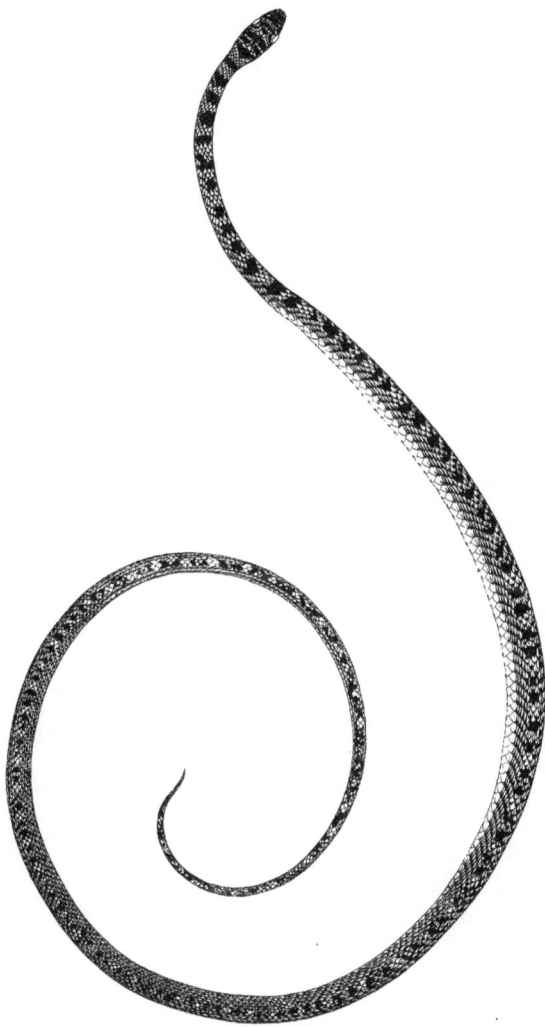

Kalla Jin. *Chrysopelea ornata* (Shaw).

Dora.

Kerril pattee. *Hydrophis nigrocinctus Daudin*
Hydris

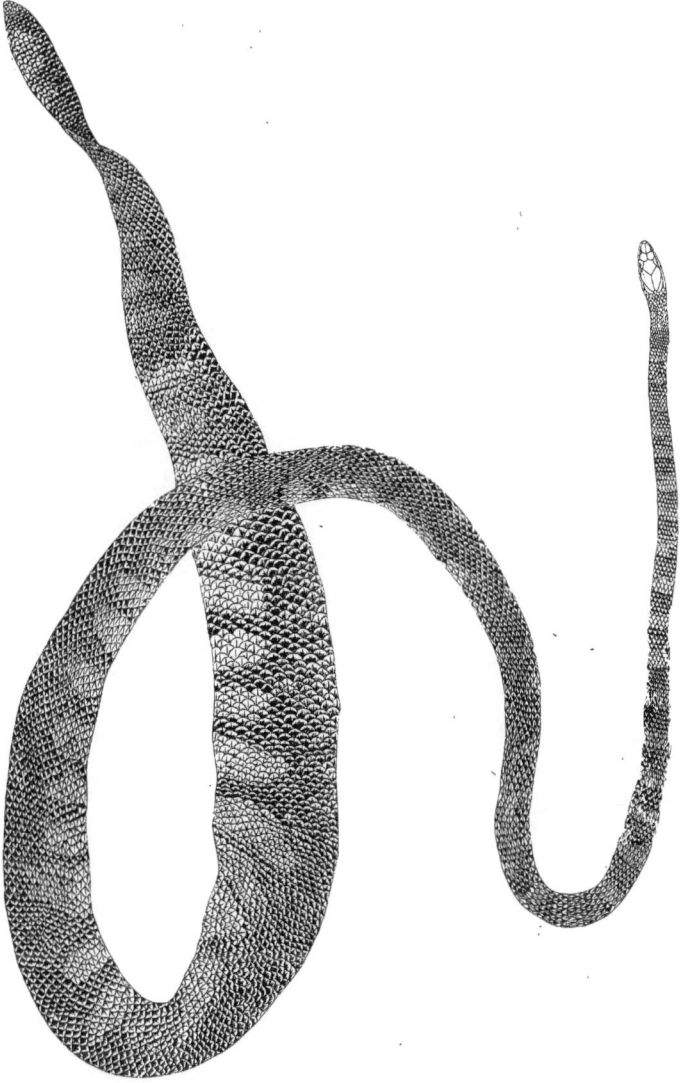

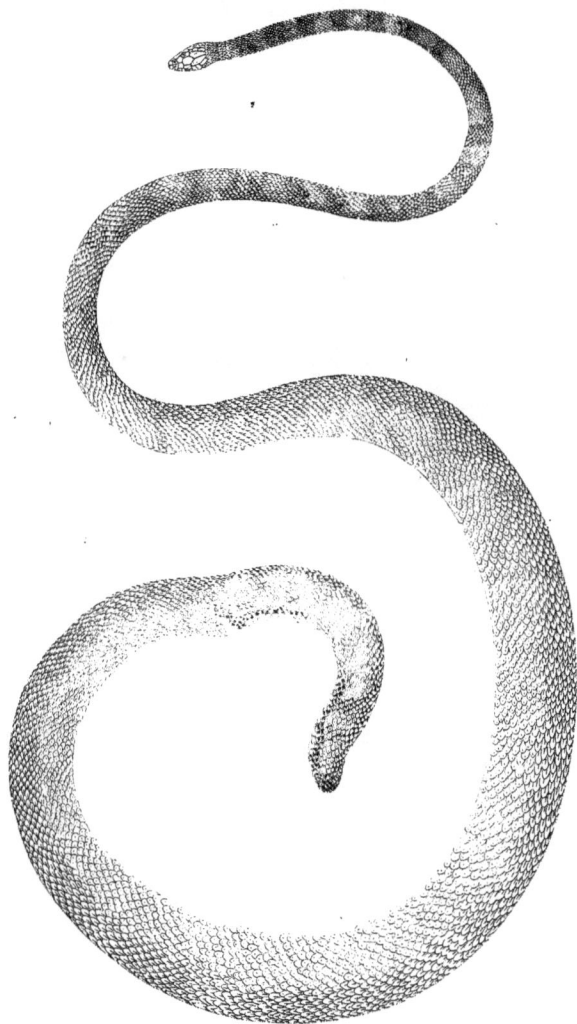

Kalla Shootur sun. *Hydrophis obscurus Daudin*
Hydrus

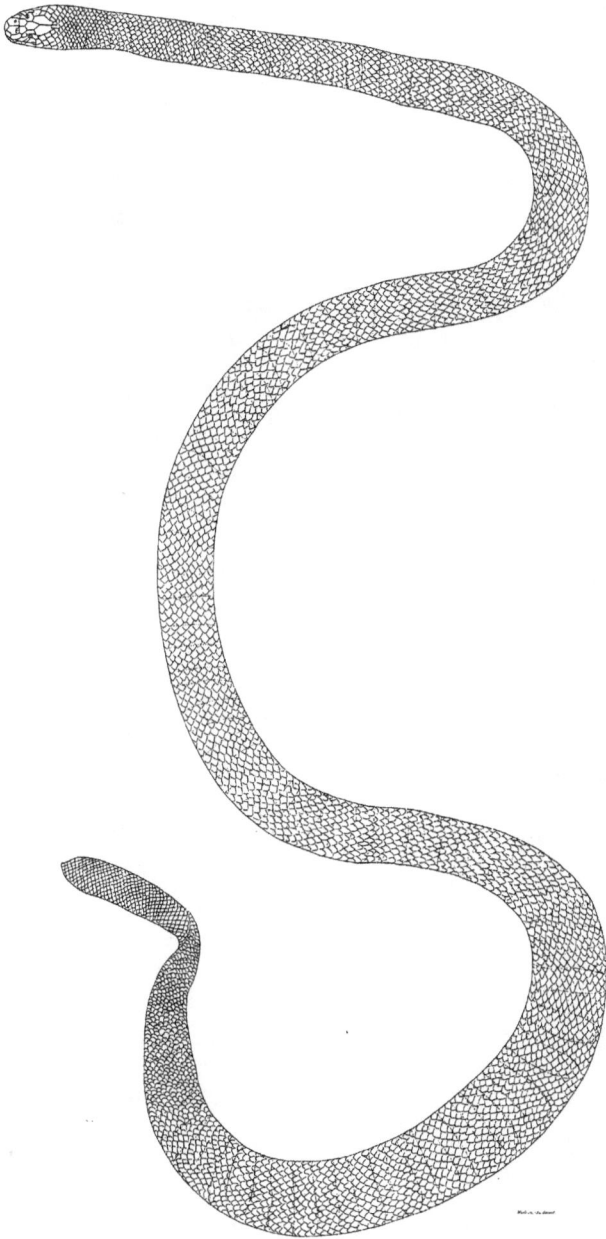

Chittul. *Distira cyanocincta* (Jardin)

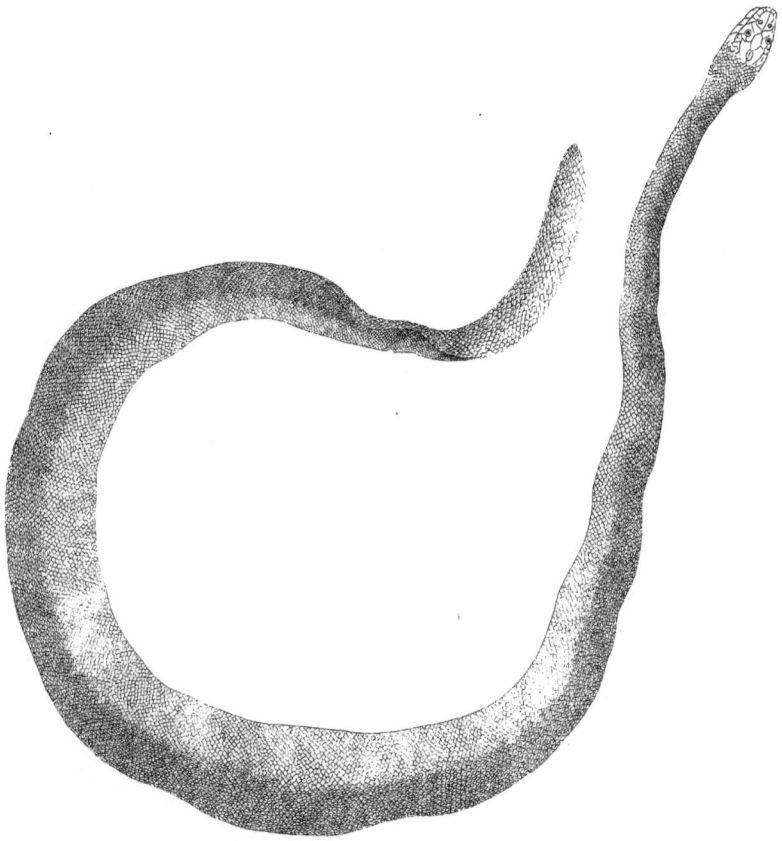

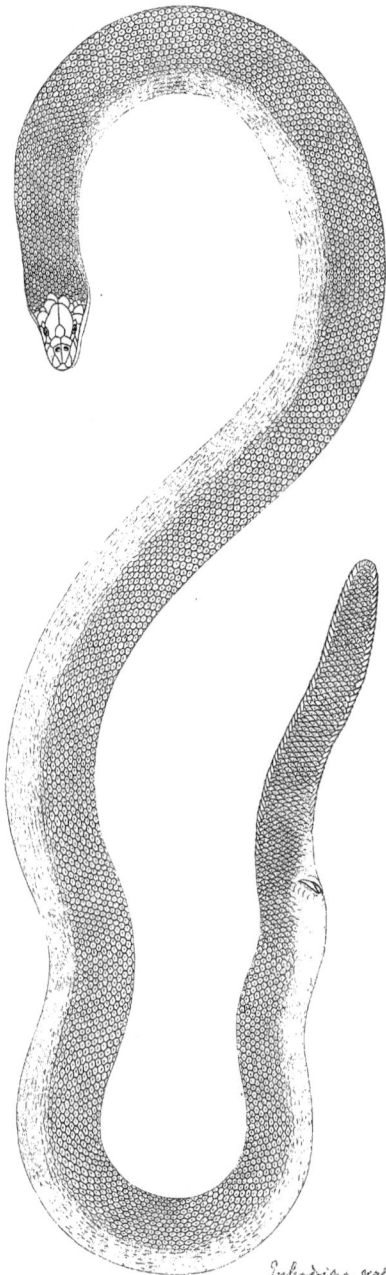

Valakadyen

Eulipdeina valakadien (Rivia) "Kram. sp."

Shiddil *Distira judonii (Gray)*

(*Hydrophis?athiceps Fink 1837 ! 44*)

XIII

Kadell Nagam
(*Hydrophis gracilis* (Shaw).

Shaw. 1pl.

Ourdia.

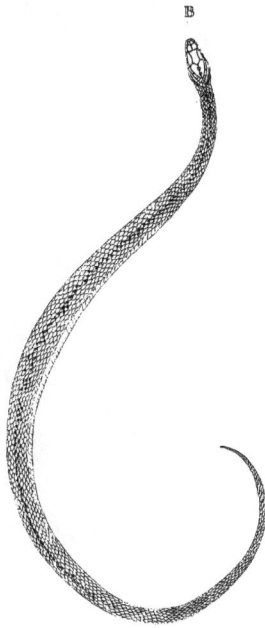

A   B

Ourdia A   Ourdia B *Tropidonotus stolatus (China)*

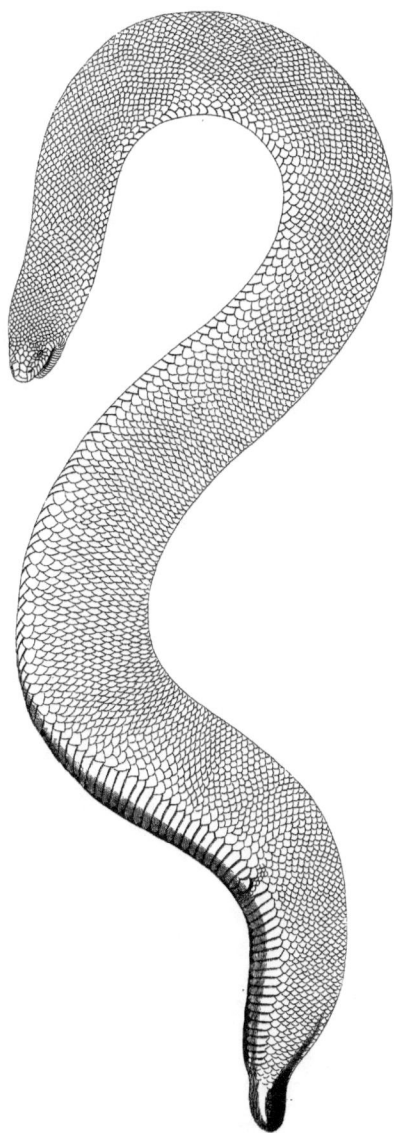

Erutaley Nagam

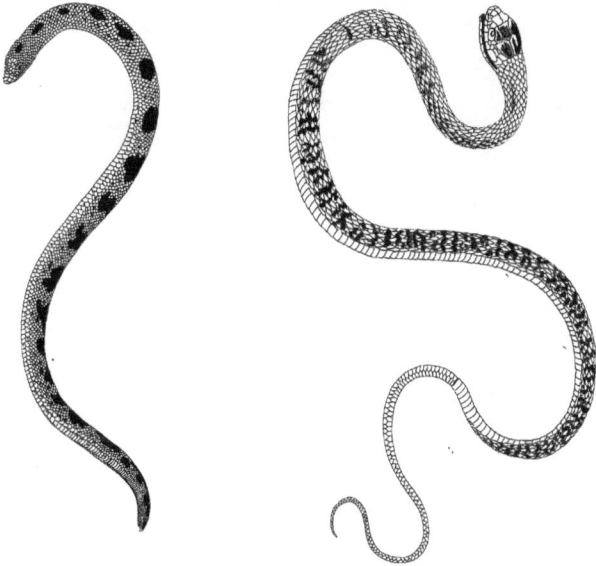

Anguilis vittata mala Naurenti
...

Ancistrodon rhodostoma (Boie)

D. ... multimaculata (Schleg.)

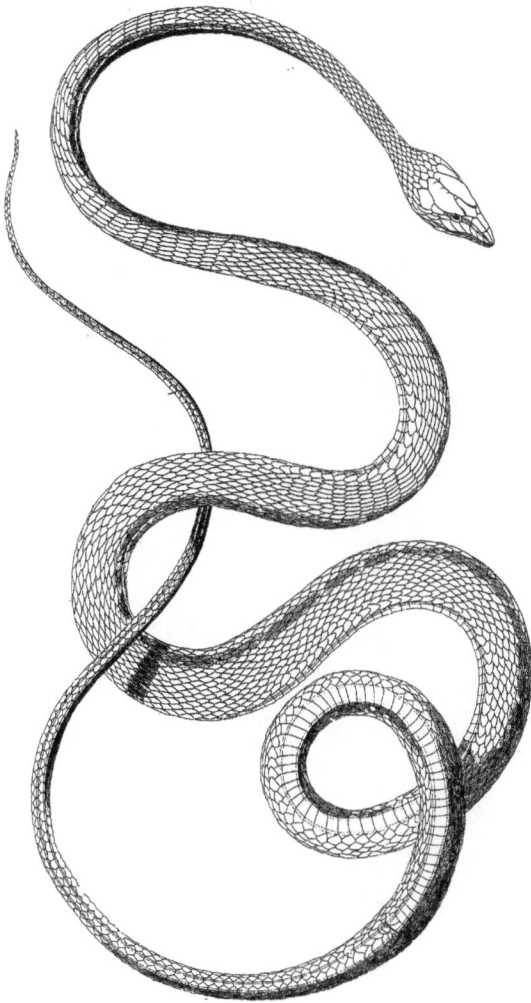

Coronella prasinus Boie.

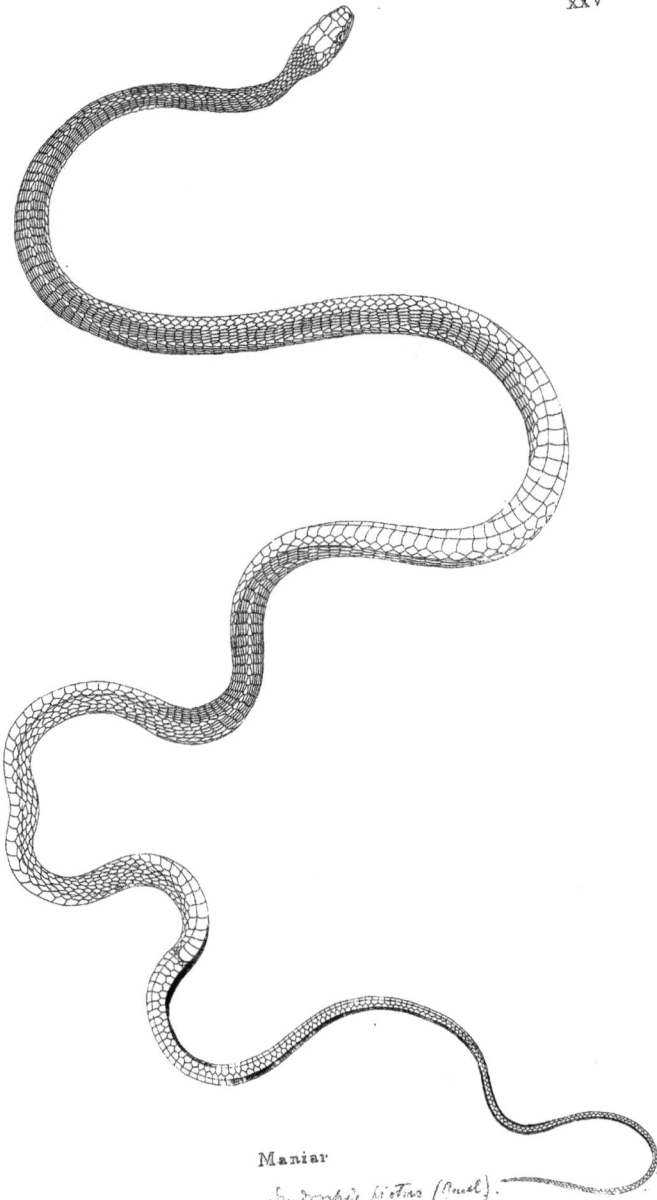

Maniar

Dendrophis pictus (Gmel.)

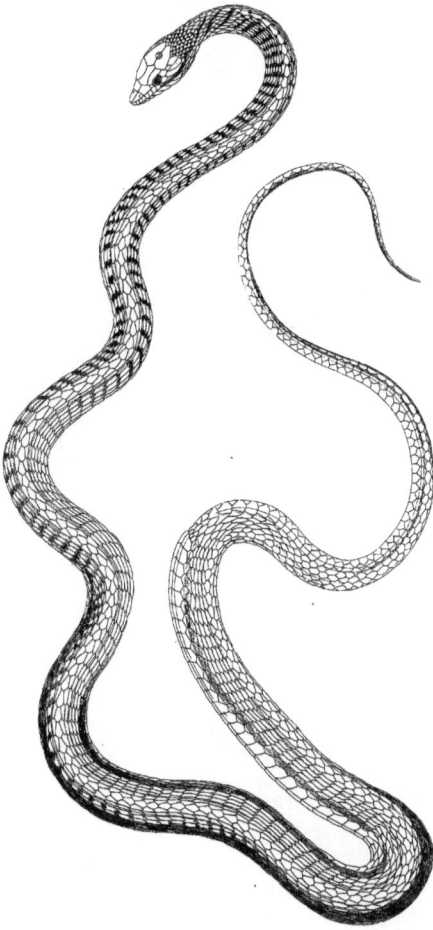

Combari Mokeen   *Dendrophis pictus (Gmel.)*

Zamenis diadema (Schleg.).

Vipera russelii (Shaw)

Homalopsis buccata (dim.)

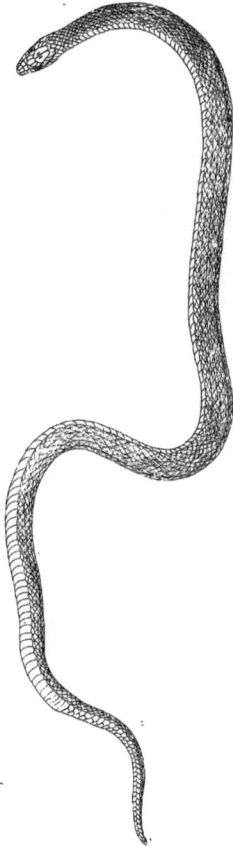

Coluber Naja

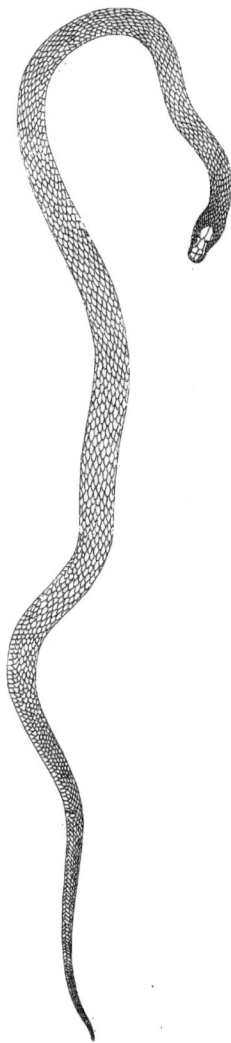

Enhydris rhynchops (Homalopsidae)

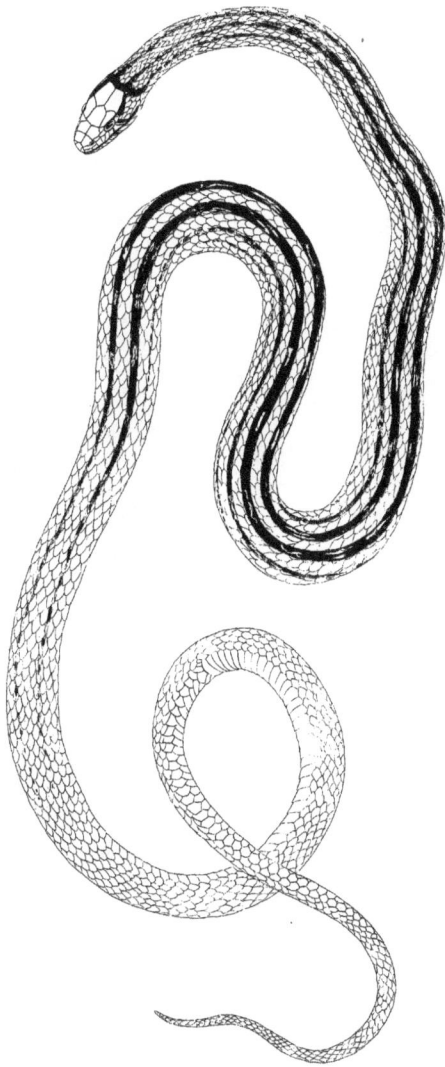

XLI

Coluber radiatus Schleg.

Fig. 1.

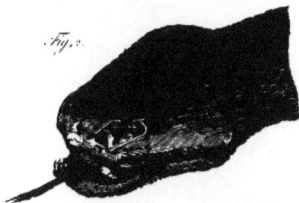

Fig. 2.

Fig. 3.

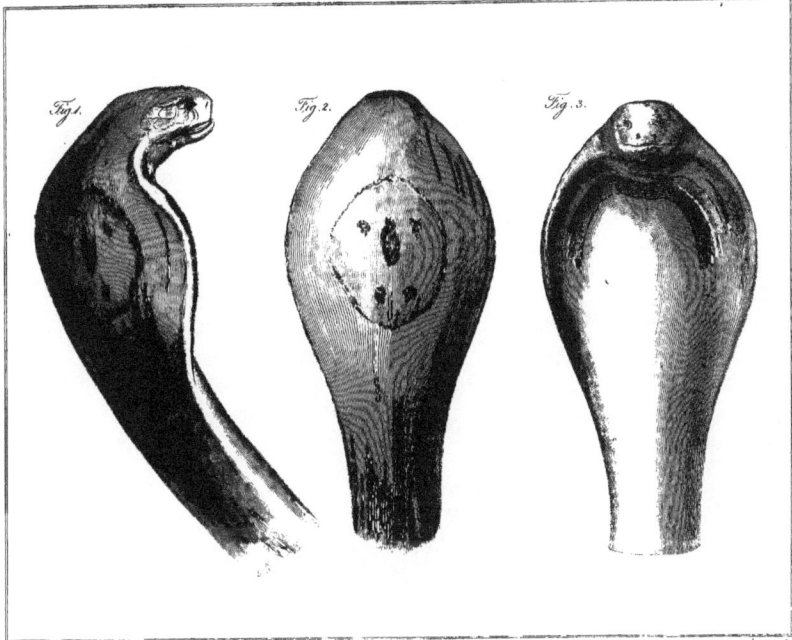

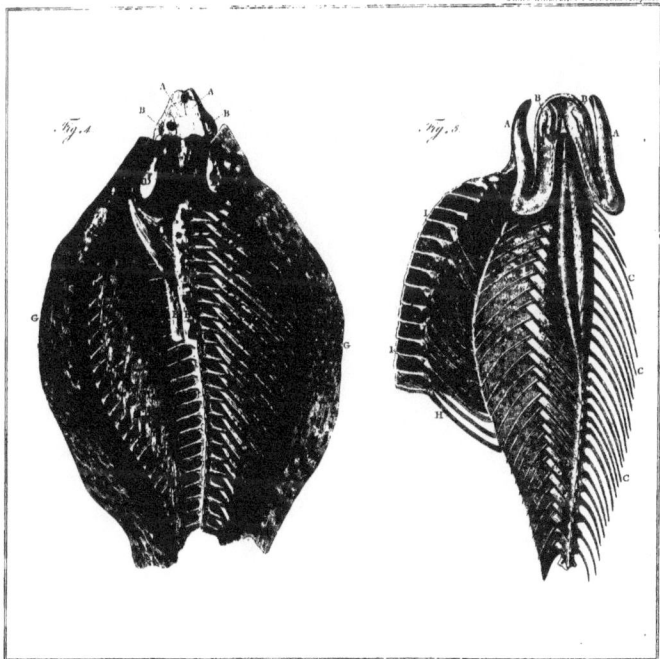

APPENDIX.

No. I.

Remarks on the Voluntary Expansion of the Skin of the Neck in the Cobra de Capello, *or Hooded Snake of the East Indies. By* PATRICK RUSSELL, *M. D. F. R. S. With a Description of the Structure of the Parts which perform that Office. By* EVERARD HOME, *Esq. F. R. S.*

Read before the ROYAL SOCIETY, June 14th, 1804.

THE remarkable expansion of the skin of the neck in the Coluber Naja of LINNÆUS, or Cobra de Capello of the East Indies, and which constitutes a principal character of the species, is produced by an apparatus, hitherto, as I believe, very imperfectly described. It is a voluntary action, totally distinct from that inflation which all serpents when irritated are more or less capable of, and which the Coluber Naja also assumes at the same time that it expands its hood.

In botanical excursions in India, fragments of serpentine skeletons, made by the black ants, were occasionally met with; but in such as were supposed to belong to the Coluber Naja, the peculiar disposition and structure of the cervical ribs, so different from that in other serpents, had escaped me.

In other serpents, the ribs from the first vertebra to those of the middle of the trunk gradually increase in length; thence they gradually shorten or decline to near the end of the tail, where they disappear or are transformed into short eminences; but in the Coluber Naja, the cervical ribs gradually lengthen to the tenth or eleventh, after which they successively shorten to the twentieth. The ribs, again increasing in length, are at the middle of the trunk, nearly as long as the middle cervical ribs, and then declining, as usual in other serpents, disappear on the tail.

So obvious a peculiarity in the skeleton of the Cobra de Capello, having escaped my notice in India, and finding myself unable to account for the expansion of its hood, which is commonly, in that country, conceived to be connected with inspiration, I brought with me, on my return to England, several subjects for dissection, in order to have the matter properly ascertained; my friend Mr. HOME readily undertook the task, and the subjoined result of his investigation will, I have no doubt, prove satisfactory.

I have on another occasion asserted as a fact, that the neck of the Cobra de Capello, in a quiescent state, shews no external protuberance whatever;* and it is clearly accounted for in the following description, from the ribs, when depressed, lying upon the spine over one another.

MR. HOME'S DESCRIPTION.

THE mechanism by which the Cobra de Capello, when irritated and ready to seize its prey, expands the skin of the neck, giving it the appearance from which the snake takes its name, consists entirely of muscles, acting upon the ribs and external skin of the animal.

From the rounded form of the hood, the skin has the appearance of being inflated; but the most careful examination did not discover any communication between the trachea or the lungs and the cellular membrane under the skin.

In this snake, the ribs nearest the head, to the number of twenty on each side, have a different shape from the rest; instead of bending equally with the other ribs towards the belly, they go out in a lateral direction, having only a slight curvature, and when depressed, lie upon the side of the spine on one another.

* Continuation of an Account of Indian Serpents, page 3.

The first rib is shorter than the rest, and they become gradually longer to the tenth and eleventh, which are the longest; they afterwards become gradually shorter to the twentieth, which is nearly of the same length as the first; so that the ribs on each side, when extended, form an oval figure, of which the spine is the middle line or long axis.

In the extended state of the ribs, the skin of the back is brought over them, forming the hood; and in their depressed state the hood disappears.

The ribs are raised by four sets of muscles: one set from the spine to the upper edge of each rib; a second set from the ribs above, passing over two ribs to the third rib below; another set have their origin from the rib above, pass over one rib, and are inserted into the second below; and a fourth set pass from rib to rib.

The combined effects of these four sets of muscles, raises and extends the ribs; their direction and appearance is so distinctly seen in the annexed figures, as to make a more particular description in a paper of this kind, unnecessary.

The skin of the back is brought forwards on the neck, by a large set of very long muscles going off from each of the first twenty ribs on each side, a quarter of an inch from their head by a tendinous origin, which soon becomes fleshy; the longest of these muscles is two inches long; they are inserted into the skin; and when the ribs have been first extended, have the power of bringing the skin forwards to a great extent. By these means the hood is formed.

To depress the ribs, and restore the parts to that state in which the neck of the animal does not appear disproportionally protuberant, but of the same size as the rest of the snake, there are three sets of muscles: one set goes from the vertebræ of the neck to the lower edge of each rib; but, to give these muscles a greater length of fibre, they are not inserted into the rib immediately above the vertebræ, but pass upwards and outwards over three ribs, and are inserted into the fourth at the middle part of it. These muscles become antagonists to those which raise the ribs.

The second set arises from the points of the ribs; and each muscle goes to be inserted into the skin nearer the head, counteracting the muscles which bring the skin forwards, and drawing it by their action back again. The third set goes from the root of one scutum to the root of the scutum immediately above it, so as to bring it down upon the other.

The object of the present paper being to explain the mechanism upon which the hood, the peculiar characteristic of this species of snake, depends, it is not meant to enter into the uses for which the hood is intended. It may not however be improper to observe, that the expansion of the ribs answers no good purpose respecting the lungs, since they are not so situated in this animal as to receive any advantage from it; but the gullet, where it passes down along the neck, admits of great expansion; and the extended state of the ribs, at the time the animal is employed in catching its prey, may give to the gullet a facility of being dilated for the reception of the food.

EXPLANATION OF THE FIGURES.

PLATE VII.

Fig. 1. A side view of the head and neck of the Cobra de Capello, drawn from the living animal.

Fig. 2. A back view of the hood.

Fig. 3. A front view of the hood.

PLATE VIII.

Fig. 4. A back view of the neck in its expanded state; the external skin being dissected off, and turned aside to shew the muscles which raise the ribs, and bring the skin forwards towards the head.

This view is intended principally to exhibit the muscles which raise the ribs, and those which, when the ribs are raised, act upon the external skin, and bring it forwards.

AA. The scales on the head of the snake.

BB. The eyes.

APPENDIX I.

49

CC. The muscles which surround the poison glands.

DD. A portion of the poison glands exposed.

EE. A pair of muscles which rise from the neck, and terminate in the head.

F. One of a pair of muscles which bring the head back.

GG. The skin divided in the middle line of the back dissected from the muscles, and turned on each side.

HH. The intercostal muscles.

II. The muscles which bring forward the skin of the back upon the neck to form the hood. They arise from the ribs, and are inserted into the skin.

KK. Muscles which raise the ribs: they originate from that part of the rib near the spine, pass over two ribs, and are inserted into the rib below near its extremity.

LL. Muscles which raise the ribs; arising from one rib and passing over the next, to be inserted into the rib below.

MM. The intercostal muscles.

Fig. 5. A front view of the neck. The parts are dissected to shew the mode in which the ribs lie in their depressed state; also the muscles by which they are depressed, and those which bring the skin back into its natural state.

AA. The two portions of the lower jaw separated from each other, and turned aside.

BB. The poison fangs.

CCC. The ribs in their depressed state lying over each other on the side of the spine.

DDD. The ribs on the opposite side in their extended state: their extremities become the boundary of the hood, and give it an oval form.

EE. A pair of muscles which bring the head forward upon the neck.

FF. The intercostal muscles.

GG. The muscles which bring the ribs downwards upon the spine.

HH. The muscles which bring the skin backwards from the neck: they have their origin from the points of the ribs, and are inserted into the lower edge of the abdominal scuta.

II. The abdominal scuta divided in the middle line of the belly.

KK. The muscles which go from the lower edge of one scutum to the lower edge of the scutum over it, to bring the scuta closer together, and make them overlap.

LL. An internal view of the skin of the snake beyond the abdominal scuta.

No. II.

Observations on the Orifices found in certain Poisonous Snakes, situated between the Nostril and the Eye. By PATRICK RUSSELL, *M. D. F. R. S. With some Remarks on the Structure of those Orifices, and the Description of a Bag connected with the Eye, met with in the same Snakes. By* EVERARD HOME, *Esq. F. R. S.*

Read before the ROYAL SOCIETY, February 2, 1804.

IN the description of the *Fer-de-lance*, or yellow snake of Martinico, the Count de la CEPEDE has remarked an orifice on each side of the head, between the nostril and the eye, which had by some naturalists been conceived to be the external organ of hearing; but not having an opportunity himself to ascertain the fact by dissection, he recommends it as an interesting object for future investigation.*

* Hist. Nat. tom. ii. p. 122.

I have, in the course of the last three years, received two Colubers from Java; and, by favour of Dr. CLARK, two from Martinico; all four venomous, and distinguished by lateral orifices. In the month of January, 1803, Dr. GARTHSHORE presented me with a specimen of the yellow snake of Martinico in excellent preservation.

Six subjects, distinguished by these lateral orifices now in my possession, offering a fair opportunity to determine a curious circumstance in comparative anatomy, the specimens were submitted to my friend Mr. HOME, of whose assistance I had more than once availed myself in similar investigations. My request was once more attended to; and the subjoined Description and Remarks were received in return.

Among the specimens submitted to Mr. HOME, was one of the *Bodroo Pam*, in the description of which, lately published,* I have misrepresented the orifices now in question as the nostrils, having intirely overlooked the real nostrils.

While the anatomical disquisitions were going on, inspection was made into some of the numerous collections of serpents preserved in the Museums in London. In the British Museum I was shewn, exclusive of the Rattle-snake and the Fer-de-lance, four or five Colubers,+ with lateral orifices; in the LEVERIAN Museum I found two or three; in the HUNTERIAN Museum, two Colubers,‡ and three Boæ;§ and in that of Mr. HEAVISIDE, one Coluber.‖

The total found in the Museums above-mentioned, (exclusive of the Rattle-snake,) were ten or eleven Colubers, and three Boæ; which, added to five Colubers in my own possession, amount to eighteen or nineteen subjects furnished with lateral orifices.

It appears on the whole, that the lateral orifices have hitherto been found only in venomous serpents.

That (exclusive of the Rattle-snake), they have been found in fifteen or sixteen species of Colubers, and in three of the Genus Boa.

That they have not as yet been discovered in any of the Genus Anguis.

Mr. HOME's investigations have clearly established that these lateral orifices in serpents, and the bags to which they lead, have no communication with the organ of hearing. Another fact ascertained by him is, that serpents distinguished by lateral orifices, have a cavity situated between the bag and the eye, which, so far as I know, has not been observed before.

MR. HOME'S DESCRIPTION AND REMARKS.

THE orifices situated between the eye and the nostril in the Rattle-snake, and in some species of Coluber, do not lead to the nostril or to the ear, but to a distinct bag of a rounded form; there is a hollow of the same shape surrounded by bone, and adapted to receive it. Dr. TYSON's description of the Rattle-snake is tolerably accurate : he says, " between the nostrils and the eyes, but somewhat lower, were two orifices which " I took for the ears, but after, I found they only led into a bone that had a pretty large cavity, but no " perforation."¶

The cavity which Dr. TYSON describes to be in the bone, is a cup, formed by the bones of the skull and those of the upper jaw; it is in shape not unlike the orbit, and is formed in a similar manner.

These bags bear a relative proportion to the size of the snake; they are lined, as also the eyelids, with a cuticle which forms the transparent cornea, making a part of the outer cuticle, and is shed with it; and, when examined after the snake has cast it off, their shape is more perfectly seen than under any other circumstances.

In the annexed figures one of these bags is represented in different views; all of them of the natural size, both in the *Fer-de-lance* or yellow snake of Martinico, and in the detached cuticle of the Rattle-snake. The appearance in the *Bodroo Pam* is exactly the same; but, as the bag in that snake is of a smaller size, it was considered unnecessary to give a representation of it.

In the deer and antelope there are bags, in the same relative situation respecting the eye and the nose,

* Account of Indian Serpents collected on the Coast of Coromandel, No. IX.   † All I believe Nondescripts.
‡ No. 977, 1058.   §.No. 893, 1016, 1046.   ‖ No. 64.   ¶ Philos. Trans. vol. xiii. p. 26.

resting upon the skull ; there is also a cavity in the bone adapted to receive them. The bags vary in size in the different species of these genera. The French naturalists have given the name of *larmiers* to these bags, conceiving them to be receptacles for the tears, of which the thinner parts evaporating, a substance remains called *larmes de cerf*.

I requested my friend Mr. ANDRE to examine these bags in the common buck, and to observe their relative position to the puncta lachrymalia ; his situation in the Earl of EGREMONT's family at Petworth affording him every opportunity for doing it. He informs me that the bags are lined with a cuticle similar to that of the meatus auditorius externus in the human ear ; their internal surface is smooth, free from hair, and without any appearance of glandular structure. From the inner angle of the eye to this bag, there is a kind of gutter in the skin, of a darker colour than the rest of the skin in light coloured animals, and the hairs are shorter than on the rest of the body : the substance contained in the bags resembled that found in the ears.

The lachrymal gland in the deer, he says, is very large, and the puncta so much so, as to admit the rounded end of a common probe. There is no lachrymal sac ; the tubes from the puncta unite and pass through a small opening in the bone to the nose.

The following account of these bags, in the Antelope of Sumatra, was transmitted to me in the year 1792, by Mr. BELL. " The external orifice is of the size of a crow quill ; it leads into a bag not larger than a " small marble, which is lined with a cuticle with hair. From this bag there is a secretion of a limpid fluid, " which keeps oozing down the nose." This gentleman, unfortunately for Natural History, died at Sumatra soon after the date of his letter.

In the HUNTERIAN Museum, intrusted by Government to the care of the College of Surgeons, there are several specimens of these bags from the Egyptian Antelope, with annulated horns, and also from some other species ; these are preserved so as to shew the internal cavity of the bag, and the structure of the gland immediately behind it. In these specimens the glandular part is one-fourth of an inch in thickness ; from the centre of this gland, an excretory duct opens into the bag immediately opposite to the external orifice. The bag itself is lined with a cuticle, and thinly set with strong hairs.

The facts now produced are sufficient to prove that these bags have a secretion of their own, the quantity of which varies according to the climate and other circumstances ; and there is no reason for thinking that the tears ever pass into them, the passage into the nose being unusually free, and the orifices in the bags in many species unfavourably situated for the reception of the tears.

We are at present unacquainted with the use to which the fluid secreted in these bags is applied.

As amphibious animals, in general, have no glands to supply the skin with moisture from within, but receive it by coming in contact with moist substances, it is possible the bags in the snake may be supplied in that manner, and the more so, as the cuticular lining appears perfect.

Another peculiarity is remarkable in snakes furnished with the bags described above, namely, an oval cavity situated between the bag and the eye, the opening into which is within the inner angle of the eyelid, and directed towards the cornea. In this opening there are two rows of projections which appear to form an orifice capable of dilatation and contraction. From the situation of these oval cavities, they must be considered as reservoirs for a fluid, which is occasionally to be spread over the cornea ; and they may be filled by the falling of the dew, or the moisture shaken off from the grass through which the snake passes.

This apparatus in the snake has that position which is best adapted to pour out the fluid upon the cornea, when the head of the snake is erect.

Dr. TYSON had superficially observed the apparatus which has been described, and considered it as a membrana nictitans. He says, " inwards it seemed to have a membrana nictitans, which removes any dust " that might adhere to the eye."*

---

* Phil. Trans. vol. xiii. p. 27.

As Snakes in general have no apparatus to wash the cornea, these particular species must have some peculiarities in their mode of life, with which we are not at present acquainted.

EXPLANATION OF THE FIGURES.

PLATE III.

Fig. 1. Represents a side view of the head of the *Fer de lance*, or Yellow Snake of Martinico, to shew the external appearance of the orifice with its relative situation to the nostril and the eye. The parts are delineated of their natural size.

Fig. 2. A side view of the head of the same Snake, in which the bag is laid open. At the aperture of the cavity, which opens towards the cornea, there is a double row of small projecting points.

Fig. 3. The cuticle of the Rattle-Snake, after it had been cast off from one side of the head, represented of its natural dimensions. In this view the internal surface only of the cuticle is seen. There is an aperture of an irregularly oval form, which is the opening of the nostril : a little farther on is the lining of the rounded bag, in a distended state ; nearer the eye is the cavity communicating with the space before the cornea, it is of an oval form, and has a narrow neck ; beyond this neck is the transparent cornea, which in the Snake is cuticular, and is shed with the external covering of the other parts. Through the transparent cornea a bristle is seen passing before its external surface into the cavity.

This figure is taken from a preparation in the HUNTERIAN MUSEUM.

No. III.

Extract from MR. HOME'S *Account of the Case of a Man who died by the Bite of a Rattle-Snake.*

Read before the ROYAL SOCIETY, December 21, 1809.

THE following cases were sent from India, to my late friend Dr. PATRICK RUSSELL : they arrived after his death, and Mr. CLAUD RUSSELL very kindly gave them to me, knowing the subject of them to be one, in which I had taken an interest.

A boy, a slave of a gentleman in India, was bitten by a snake called Kamulee by the natives, in the lower part of the arm, at eight o'clock in the evening. The blood flowed very freely for some time. He died next day at noon in great pain.

A sepoy, 60 years of age, was admitted into the hospital of his regiment, under the care of Mr. PERRIN, assistant surgeon, at four o'clock in the afternoon of the 15th of October, 1802, in consequence of his being bitten by a Cobra di Capello, on the back part of the hand. At the time of his admission he complained of pain running up the arm. He immediately took a drachm of eau de luce, and this dose was repeated every half hour, and the same remedy was applied externally as a lotion to the arm and forearm. At four o'clock in the morning of the 16th of October, the pain began to increase, and the arm to swell with great hardness and stiffness, and tumor in the axilla, with much inclination to vomit. He took twelve grains of Dr. JAMES's powder, which brought up a great quantity of bilious matter. He drank copiously of warm water, but no perspiration was induced. He appeared relieved for a short time. At eight o'clock in the morning the arm was distended, painful, and discoloured. He took four ounces of brandy, and repeated it every hour until twelve o'clock, with a drachm of eau de luce occasionally. At this time he was a little revived. The brandy was reduced to two ounces, which were carefully and regularly given every hour, until twelve at noon on the 17th of October, when the arm was more free from pain, but much swelled, hard, and black : his spirits and pulse also were considerably relieved. The eau de luce was now omitted, but the brandy was continued every hour, until twelve o'clock at noon on the 18th of October, when the stiffness and tumor in the axilla had disappeared: the arm was still swelled, but was softer, and less painful. The brandy was omitted : at night he took six grains of Dr. JAMES's powder. On the 19th of October the arm was less, softer, with little or no pain; a blister was formed and burst on the back of the hand, which discharged three ounces of black fœtid pus. On the 20th, an abscess burst on the hand, in the same situation as the blister, which discharged a large quantity of a fluid having an offensive smell. He was directed to take a drachm of Peruvian bark in port wine, every two hours. On the 22d the swelling was gone, but the discharge was considerable. From this time the man gradually, but slowly recovered, with the loss of the use of his forefinger, which remained permanently extended, and some of the other fingers were affected in a less degree.

In this case, the swelling of the arm was slower in coming on, and less extensive ; the pain running up to the axilla, which preceded it, was mistaken for the effect of absorption.

INDEX.

INDEX.

PART II. CONTINUATION OF INDIAN SERPENTS.

INDEX.

ANGUIS.

PART I. COAST OF COROMANDEL.

PART II. CONTINUATION OF INDIAN SERPENTS.

London : Printed by W. Bulmer and Co.
Cleveland-row, St. James's.